S0-BOG-617

DEMCO

Jerry Spinelli

WHO
WROTE
THAT?

LOUISA MAY ALCOTT

JANE AUSTEN

AVI

JUDY BLUME,
    SECOND EDITION

BETSY BYARS

BEVERLY CLEARY

ROBERT CORMIER

BRUCE COVILLE

ROALD DAHL

CHARLES DICKENS

THEODOR GEISEL

S.E. HINTON

WILL HOBBS

ANTHONY HOROWITZ

STEPHEN KING

MADELEINE L'ENGLE

GAIL CARSON LEVINE

C.S. LEWIS

LOIS LOWRY

ANN M. MARTIN

L.M. MONTGOMERY

PAT MORA

WALTER DEAN MYERS

SCOTT O'DELL

BARBARA PARK

GARY PAULSEN

RICHARD PECK

TAMORA PIERCE

EDGAR ALLAN POE

BEATRIX POTTER

PHILIP PULLMAN

MYTHMAKER:
    THE STORY OF
    J.K. ROWLING,
    SECOND EDITION

MAURICE SENDAK

SHEL SILVERSTEIN

JERRY SPINELLI

R.L. STINE

EDWARD L.
    STRATEMEYER

E.B. WHITE

LAURA INGALLS
    WILDER

LAURENCE YEP

JANE YOLEN

WHO
WROTE
THAT?

Jerry Spinelli

Tracey Baptiste

Foreword by
Kyle Zimmer

CHELSEA HOUSE
PUBLISHERS
An imprint of Infobase Publishing

Jerry Spinelli

Chelsea House
An imprint of Infobase Publishing
132 West 31st Street
New York NY 10001

Library of Congress Cataloging-in-Publication Data
Baptiste, Tracey.
Jerry Spinelli / Tracey Baptiste.
p. cm. — (Who wrote that?)
Includes bibliographical references and index.
ISBN 978-0-7910-9572-0 (acid-free paper) 1. Spinelli, Jerry—Juvenile literature. 2. Authors, American—20th century—Biography—Juvenile literature. 3. Young adult fiction—Authorship—Juvenile literature. I. Title. II. Series.
PS3569.P546Z59 2009
813'.54—dc22
[B]
                            2008035037

Chelsea House books are available at special discounts when purchased in bulk quantities for business, associations, institutions, or sales promotions. Please call our Special Sales Department in New York at (212) 967-8800 or (800) 322-8755.

You can find Chelsea House on the World Wide Web at http://www.chelseahouse.com

Text design by Keith Trego
Cover design by Alicia Post

Printed in the United States of America

Bang EJB 10 9 8 7 6 5 4 3 2 1

This book is printed on acid-free paper.

All links and Web addresses were checked and verified to be correct at the time of publication. Because of the dynamic nature of the Web, some addresses and links may have changed since publication and may no longer be valid.

Table of Contents

FOREWORD BY
KYLE ZIMMER
PRESIDENT, FIRST BOOK

HUMANITY IS POWERED by stories. From our earliest days as thinking beings, we employed every available tool to tell each other stories. We danced, drew pictures on the walls of our caves, spoke, and sang. All of this extraordinary effort was designed to entertain, recount the news of the day, explain natural occurrences—and then gradually to build religious and cultural traditions and establish the common bonds and continuity that eventually formed civilizations. Stories are the most powerful force in the universe; they are the primary element that has distinguished our evolutionary path.

Our love of the story has not diminished with time. Enormous segments of societies are devoted to the art of storytelling. Book sales in the United States alone topped $24 billion in 2006; movie studios spend fortunes to create and promote stories; and the news industry is more pervasive in its presence than ever before.

There is no mystery to our fascination. Great stories are magic. They can introduce us to new cultures, or remind us of the nobility and failures of our own, inspire us to greatness or scare us to death; but above all, stories provide human insight on a level that is unavailable through any other source. In fact, stories connect each of us to the rest of humanity not just in our own time, but also throughout history.

This special magic of books is the greatest treasure that we can hand down from generation to generation. In fact, that spark in a child that comes from books became the motivation for the creation of my organization, First Book, a national literacy program with a simple mission: to provide new books to the most disadvantaged children. At present, First Book has been at work in hundreds of communities for over a decade. Every year children in need receive millions of books through our organization and millions more are provided through dedicated literacy institutions across the United States and around the world. In addition, groups of people dedicate themselves tirelessly to working with children to share reading and stories in every imaginable setting from schools to the streets. Of course, this Herculean effort serves many important goals. Literacy translates to productivity and employability in life and many other valid and even essential elements. But at the heart of this movement are people who love stories, love to read, and want desperately to ensure that no one misses the wonderful possibilities that reading provides.

When thinking about the importance of books, there is an overwhelming urge to cite the literary devotion of great minds. Some have written of the magnitude of the importance of literature. Amy Lowell, an American poet, captured the concept when she said, "Books are more than books. They are the life, the very heart and core of ages past, the reason why men lived and worked and died, the essence and quintessence of their lives." Others have spoken of their personal obsession with books, as in Thomas Jefferson's simple statement: "I live for books." But more compelling, perhaps, is the almost instinctive excitement in children for books and stories.

Throughout my years at First Book, I have heard truly extraordinary stories about the power of books in the lives of children. In one case, a homeless child, who had been bounced from one location to another, later resurfaced—and the only possession that he had fought to keep was the book he was given as part of a First Book distribution months earlier. More recently, I met a child who, upon receiving the book he wanted, flashed a big smile and said, "This is my big chance!" These snapshots reveal the true power of books and stories to give hope and change lives.

As these children grow up and continue to develop their love of reading, they will owe a profound debt to those volunteers who reached out to them—a debt that they may repay by reaching out to spark the next generation of readers. But there is a greater debt owed by all of us—a debt to the storytellers, the authors, who have bound us together, inspired our leaders, fueled our civilizations, and helped us put our children to sleep with their heads full of images and ideas.

WHO WROTE THAT? is a series of books dedicated to introducing us to a few of these incredible individuals. While we have almost always honored stories, we have not uniformly honored storytellers. In fact, some of the most important authors have toiled in complete obscurity throughout their lives or have been openly persecuted for the uncomfortable truths that they have laid before us. When confronted with the magnitude of their written work or perhaps the daily grind of our own, we can forget that writers are people. They struggle through the same daily indignities and dental appointments, and they experience the intense joy and bottomless despair that many of us do. Yet somehow they rise above it all to deliver a powerful thread that connects us all. It is a rare honor to have the opportunity that these books provide to share the lives of these extraordinary people. Enjoy.

Above, a painting by Frank Batson depicting Norristown, Pennsylvania, as it was during Jerry Spinelli's childhood in the 1940s.

1

All the Whats a Kid Could Be

THE EAST END

George E. Spinelli was born on February 1, 1941, in Norristown, Pennsylvania. Right away, his Aunt Margaret decided he looked more like a Jerry than a George. Everybody called him Jerry after that. You'll barely find any reference to George E. Spinelli other than on his college records.

Jerry's first home was in a redbrick house on Marshall Street in the east end of town. The Spinellis lived in the second-floor apartment, and two other families occupied the first and third floors. Every night, the family that lived above Jerry's family would go through the Spinellis' apartment to their bedrooms above. Behind the house, the Adam Scheidt Brewing Company provided the permanent smell of sour, slightly rotting hops. The sounds that filled the night air were the air raid sirens of the 1940s, reminding everyone that in Europe, Asia, and Africa, soldiers were fighting World War II. At night, a train chugged along the tracks and spat coal-clogged steam into the air. The coal settled and covered everything. The sound of the chugging train worried the Spinellis' sleep.

The east end of Norristown was home to mainly Italian-American and African-American families. Jerry's grandfather, Alessandro "Alex" Spinelli, had immigrated to the United States from Italy and settled in Norristown's east end. How his grandfather came to the United States filled the younger Spinelli with wonder. To this day, he describes it like this: "He came over on a boat all by himself when he was only 14 years old."[1] Perhaps even more remarkably, Alex was an orphan. An aunt bought him a one-way steamship ticket and arranged for relatives to meet him when he arrived in America.

Jerry admired his grandfather greatly. He tried to eat chicken with his fingers like his grandfather and tried to imagine his bald grandfather as a black-haired teen who traveled by steamship to a new country. He fondly remembers the grandfather who always sat at the head of the table and drank red wine from his own barrel.

The east end, though, was more than just a place where Jerry's family lived. It was a whole world unto itself. It was a place where balls were forever being lost in landladies' backyards. The east end was home to Chatlin's department store where parents took their kids when their shoes wore out. Chatlin's had a device called a fluoroscope that took an

X-ray of the kids' feet inside the new shoes. Then the salesman and parent could determine if the desired shoes had enough wiggle room for their new owner. It was also where a patron's money and receipts were carried, fast as a shot, up and down chutes at Yost's dry goods store.

Dr. Winters's office was also in the east end. Dr. Winters was Mrs. Spinelli's dentist. He was also black. Spinelli remembers sitting in the examination chair as a three- or four-year-old as the dentist gave him an examination. The memory as he describes it is of "Dr. Winters' finger in my mouth. I can feel it, I can see its dark brownness. I notice that it is a color different from my own, but that's all there is to it, a flat, casual observation."[2] This casual observation became etched in Jerry's mind and would resurface years later in his book *Maniac Magee.* There, he describes Amanda Beale's mother with her finger in Maniac's mouth in the kitchen.

MEET THE FAMILY

On July 29, 1945, when Jerry was four and a half, his younger brother, Bill, was born. At that point, his mother had to split her time taking care of the two boys. After his brother's birth, Jerry spent much of his time with his father talking about sports. Before the boys came along, though, Mr. and Mrs. Spinelli had their own memorable moments.

Louis Anthony "Poppy" Spinelli met Lorna Mae Bigler in 1933 at a dance. He was immediately attracted to the smiling girl with dark hair. "See that girl. That's who I'm going to marry,"[3] he told a friend. On the night of May 16, 1936, he finally did. That same night, the couple wound up at another dance, where Lorna won a contest for "prettiest lady." Her prize was a photograph of herself. Later on, photos of toddlers Jerry and Bill joined her prize photo on her dresser.

Lou Spinelli, a sports fan, worked as a typesetter for Hartenstine Printing, where he had the tedious task of creating words one lead letter at a time. He also collected tickets at football games and kept score at basketball games. As soon as Jerry was old enough, his father began to take him to Norristown High School—football, basketball, and even track. Jerry took his sports very seriously: There were soccer and football in the fall, basketball in the winter, and baseball all summer. While Jerry was learning to play each sport, he was also laying the foundation to describe each of the sports-loving characters that appear in his books. Long after the game was done, he would replay the events in his mind. In those moments, he was learning to become a writer.

THE WEST END

After a brief stay on Chestnut Street, living in a house next door to his grandparents, Jerry and his family moved across the tracks. Their home for the next 10 years was on George Street in the west end of Norristown. Because they moved

Did you know...

Besides sports, Spinelli was interested in a lot of things as a young boy. Today, his interests include tennis, astronomy, country music, traveling, and spending time with his 16 grandchildren.

A photo of Spinelli's parents, Louis Anthony "Poppy" Spinelli and Lorna Mae Bigler, on their wedding day in 1936. When the couple met three years earlier, Louis was immediately convinced he had found the girl he was going to marry.

in the middle of Jerry's first year of school, he had to transfer to a new school, John F. Hartranft Elementary. He later attended Stewart Junior High School. Hartranft and Stewart were lucky to have Jerry. He was a self-described "good boy." He had perfect attendance and never misbehaved in class. He was even allowed to raise the school flag. It is sad for his fans that he was so good, because he believed that the best stories were always from the kids who got in trouble. Perhaps this is why so many of his stories are told from the perspective of the so-called bad kid. Because he was the good boy, there are not many elementary school stories of his to tell. One particular story though, did not come about from his being bad, but simply being bold. It happened this way:

On one otherwise normal day when Jerry was in the third grade, he got dressed in full cowboy gear: hat, boots, spurs, guns, and studded shirt. He walked the three blocks to school, probably clinking and clanking all the way. His teacher, Miss Davis, smiled and asked if he had something to share. Jerry got up and began to sing the song "(I Got Spurs That) Jingle Jangle Jingle" while shaking his boots for music. He said that, at the time, "I wanted to be a cowboy, and when I woke up that morning, I guess I just couldn't wait one day longer." [4] This may be one of the boldest things that Jerry did in his young life. Although he admired the daring of others in defying the rules and being the cutup in class, he rarely ever laughed loudly or even colored outside the lines.

By junior high school, Jerry's spotless attendance record had given him a string of medals almost as long as his lapel. He was also the sixth-grade spelling bee champion and the winner of several Palmer Method penmanship certificates. His experience with fighting with other boys was limited to Robert Lee "socking" him on the chin on the playground. Then, years later, he clipped Joey Stackhouse on the chin on the way home from school. Both fights were one-hit wonders. In each case, the boys wondered why they happened at all. Years later, Spinelli recalled these fights in the 1998 book *Loser*.

Because he was good student who had almost never gotten into a fight, it is surprising to discover that Jerry once talked back to a teacher. It was ninth grade. The homeroom teacher announced that she would be checking lockers for neatness. While others tidied up, Jerry went home. He was not worried because his locker was always neat. The next day, on the blackboard, were the names of the students with messy lockers. Jerry was on the list. He had to clean up his locker and got detention. He protested, knowing that there must have been a mistake. He informed his teacher that he would not show up for detention after school. Instead, he went to baseball practice. The next morning, he found that his teacher had him thrown off the team and all the privileges he had for being such a good boy had been taken away from him. He immediately apologized to the homeroom teacher, and everything went back to normal. In his autobiography, Spinelli admitted that he wished he had the courage to stand up for what he considered an injustice, but the thought of having something bad on his record for the entire school year was simply too much to bear.

The good boy may have obeyed the rules and colored inside the lines, but he was also an explorer. Fortunately for his fans, it is the explorer in him—the observations he made in his childhood—that created the details of his stories. In *Maniac Magee,* Norristown is called Two Mills, and DeKalb Street, a main street in Norristown, is Hector Street. In *Maniac Magee*, there is an east end and a west end. Black families live on one end of town and white families on the other. Marshall Street, the location of Jerry's first house, became Sycamore Street, where the character Maniac moves in with the Beales. The ash field where young Jerry played baseball is the location of Maniac's famous frog ball hit.

In an interview on the Web site AOL Kids Reads, Spinelli recalled how "the first fifteen years of my life turned out to be one big research project. I thought I was simply growing up in Norristown, Pennsylvania; looking back now I can see that I was also gathering material that would one day find its way into my books." [5] Jerry Spinelli the boy may have been born on the east end of Norristown, but Jerry Spinelli the writer seems to have sprung from the world beyond the dead end on George Street.

There were wonders on the east end. There was the field of ashes where Jerry played baseball. To the left, there was the spear field, which was a field of weeds that no one seemed able to get rid of. Above the weeds, encroaching on left field was a dump, and to the right was "Red Hill," named for the mounds of red clay it was made of. If Jerry walked north, he would cross the tracks and come to another dump and then to Stony Creek, where he was once attacked by several leeches.

More important than these wonders was what Jerry did when he was among them. He was never at a loss for something to do when he was alone: He loved to explore, and that was a solitary enterprise. Norristown has an excellent zoo, but outside of the zoo, at Stony Creek, there were frogs that hopped unseen and snakes that disappeared in the sun-speckled water. Once, he found a fat black snake and brought it home. The next day it was gone. His neighbors were scared and his mother was upset. Was it an adder? Spinelli never tells. He also became quite an expert at finding salamanders. Once, he brought home a couple of fistfuls of those poor animals. Unfortunately, he did not learn how to take care of them properly and they all died under his watch. It was a lesson that he learned the hard way.

There were other things to consider besides the animals of Stony Creek, like time and space. Spinelli says that he "tried to imagine, tried to grasp the speed of light. One hundred eighty-six thousand miles per *second!*"[6] He wondered at the stars and how many billions more there were past visible sight. He thought about what the end of the universe looked like and what would happen if he took a spaceship past the last star. He tried to grasp what there was before time.

In an interview on February 26, 2002, Spinelli told Authors Live that he has been "keeping an eye out for a good science fiction idea."[7] That eye may well have been open since his wanderings through Norristown.

In *Knots in My Yo-Yo String*, Spinelli described his wanderings by listing all the "whats" he was when he was a kid:

> So many careers came and went through me: salamander finder, crawfish annoyer, flat-stone creek skipper, cedar chest smeller, railroad car counter, tin can stomper, milkweed blower, mulberry picker, snowball smoother, paper bag popper, steel rail walker, box turtle toucher, dark-sky watcher, best-part saver. They didn't last long, these careers of mine, but flashed into and out of existence like mayflies. But while they employed me, I gave them an honest minute's work and was paid in the satisfactions of curiosity met and a job well done.[8]

Spinelli got more than just satisfaction. He was paid in the ideas of a future writer.

A photo of Jerry Spinelli in his little league uniform. An all-around athlete and popular student in middle and high school, he began to turn his attention to writing when he realized he didn't have the natural gifts to become a professional athlete.

2

The Poet

BIG SHOT

In middle school, adolescence came at Jerry fast. One day he was riding past a friend's house and was invited in to play "truth or consequences." The consequence was always that a boy had to kiss a girl. Jerry wished that he had simply ridden by, but there he was, facing a forced first kiss—and a public one at that. He had no choice. When it was over, he decided that it was not so bad after all.

His first serious relationship was with Judy Pierson. They walked everywhere together, and she had the habit of writing him block-lettered notes almost daily. Most of them involved inquiries about his mood or wished him luck at his many sporting events.

Jerry also threw his hat in the school's political ring. Both Jerry and his friend Bob Peterson decided to run for class president. On election night, Bob was nowhere to be found, but Jerry waited along with a few others after school for the results. When he was announced as the winner, Jerry was genuinely embarrassed. He was glad, but he felt badly for the other candidates. He need not have worried. After he mumbled apologies to those he had defeated, they shook his hand with praise and he walked home. On the way, he passed Bob Peterson sitting on the stoop of a girl's house. They were making out. Bob asked if Jerry had heard the results of the vote. Jerry lied, saying that he had not: He didn't have the heart to disappoint his friend. He continued on his way home.

Suddenly, Jerry was—as he put it years later—a "big shot." By the end of the ninth grade, he was "one of those kids with a couple inches of activities under [his] name in

Did you know...

Spinelli's favorites:

Book: *Wanda's Monster* by his wife, Eileen

Movie: *Anne of Green Gables*

Subject in school: Geography

Food: Ben and Jerry's New York Super Fudge Chunk ice cream in a waffle cone/chocolate almond ice cream the yearbook."[1] He was class president, an admired athlete, and class valedictorian (the student with the highest grade point average); was voted most popular boy; and had a pretty girlfriend writing him daily notes. He and his girlfriend were even voted prom king and queen. He had a beloved dog and his beloved George Street. Even the best of rides have to end sometime, though.

NOBODY

In an interview with Authors Live, Spinelli told a fan that the most difficult part of his childhood was "going from being a big shot in junior high to a nobody in high school."[2] His year in tenth grade delivered blow after blow. Sometime during that year, his family moved to the north end of Norristown, away from all the places and people Jerry loved. His girlfriend broke up with him, delivering a final note that said that they should take a little time away from each other. His aptitude for ninth-grade algebra was replaced with a complete inability to understand tenth-grade geometry. The kid who claimed to be "raised practically in a locker room"[3] watched as all of his sports dreams began to fade. He lost his speed at track, he wasn't tall enough to play basketball, and he wasn't bulky enough to be a football player. Perhaps his most hurtful sports loss was losing the ability to hit a curveball. In an interview with AOL Kidsreads.com, he described his downward slump in baseball: "I had no equal when it came to standing at shortstop and chattering to my pitcher: 'C'mon, baby, hum the pea.' Unfortunately, when I stood at the plate, so many peas were hummed past me for strikes that I decided to let somebody else become shortstop for the Yankees."[4] Years later, he still described himself not as an author but as a "failed shortstop and a grandfather who writes."[5]

To add insult to injury, he even lost his dog, Lucky. Their new home was near the highway, and Lucky wasn't used to crossing busy streets. It was Jerry's brother Bill who found the dog in the street. By the time Jerry arrived, Lucky was dead.

A new path was opening up for Jerry, though, but he could not have realized it at the time.

POETRY IN MOTION

In the sixth grade, Jerry had been asked to do a scrapbook of Mexico. He pasted pictures he found in *National Geographic* and had his father do a cover for him at the print shop, but he added one extra touch that was not part of the assignment: He wrote a poem. It was "three stanzas about Mexico, ending with a touristy come-on: 'Now isn't that where you would like to be?'" Spinelli recalls it as the first time he had ever written anything creative like a poem. "I got in trouble because the teacher didn't think I wrote it,"[6] he said in an interview for the *Washington Post*. Jerry's mother had to convince the teacher that he really had written it himself. Five years later, he chose to write another poem without being asked to do it. This time, there was no question that he was the author.

It was a Friday evening, October 11, 1957. The Norristown High football team was playing the undefeated Lower Merion. It came down to Norristown trying to hold the line one yard away from the goal. The Lower Merion fans began to celebrate because there was no way Norristown could hold the line. Meanwhile, Norristown fans sat glumly, waiting for the inevitable Lower Merion win. Then the unbelievable happened: The Norristown players held off the opposing team and the game ended 7-6, Norristown Eagles. The celebration was loud and lasted long into the night. Jerry celebrated with his friends, but

Student Waxes Poetic —

Tribute to NHS Goal-Line Stand Chronicled by Jerry Spinelli

Sixteen-year-old Jerry Spinelli, a junior student at Norristown High School, took pen in hand after last Friday night's 7-6 win over Lower Merion and paid tribute to the great NHS goal-line stand.

Spinelli, son of Mr. and Mrs. Louis A. Spinelli, 1810 Locust St., titled his clever contribution, 'Goal to Go.'

Here it is:

GOAL TO GO

The score stood seven-six
With but five minutes left to go
The Ace attack employed all tricks
To settle down its stubborn foe.

It looked as though the game was done
When an Ace stepped wide 'round right
An Eagle stopped him on the one
And tumult filled the night.

Thirty-two had come their way
And thirty-two had died
Should number thirty-three, this day
For one yard, be denied?

Roy Kent, the Eagle mentor, said,
"I've waited for this game,
And now, defense, go, stop 'em dead
And crash the Hall of Fame.

The first Ace bolted for the goal
And nothing did he see
But Branca, swearing on his soul.
"You shall not pass by me."

The next two plays convinced all
The ref would make the touchdown sign
But when the light shone on the ball
It still lay inches from the line.

Said Captain Eastwood to his gents,
"It's up to us to stop this drive."
Said Duckworth, Avery, Knerr and Spence,
"Will do, as long as we're alive."

The halfback drove with all his might
His legs were jet-propelled
But when the dust had cleared the fight
The Eagle-line had held.

— Jerry Spinelli

Above, a copy of "Goal to Go," a poem that became Spinelli's first published piece of writing. It was published alongside sportswriter Felix "Red" McCarthy's column in the Norristown Times Herald *in 1957.*

the game had not ended for him. In the morning, Jerry wrote a title: "Goal to Go." Then he wrote a poem laid out in eight rhyming verses about the game, the excitement of the day, and the emotions and determination of the players. Spinelli says that he felt "as though that goal line stand did not totally happen until I wrote the poem about it. Then, bam, the experience was over; it was completed; it was wrapped up."[7]

He gave the poem to his father, who was a longtime Norristown High School football fan. He didn't think anything of it past that point. For him, the game was finally over once he had written the last line of his poem. He did not know that his father would take it to the *Times Herald,* the local newspaper. The paper published a weekly column written by Felix "Red" McCarthy, who was Jerry's favorite writer at the time. It must have been quite an honor when he found out that McCarthy himself was responsible for having Jerry's poem appear in the sports section of the *Times Herald* on the following day. It was printed under the words "Student Waxes Poetic."

At school, classmates and teachers alike told him how much they admired the piece. Jerry was, once again, briefly in the spotlight that he had lost at the end of ninth grade. More important, he had discovered a talent that didn't have a height, weight, or batting average requirement. He decided right then that he would become a writer. "If I could've hit the curveball better, I might not have given up," he told an interviewer for the article "Writing: Spinelli Style."[8] If he had been able to hit that curveball, though, readers wouldn't have the many wonderful stories that Spinelli has written over his career. Besides, who needs another Yankee shortstop anyway? There's only one Jerry Spinelli. As a teenager, he could not have known what kind of writer he was going to become or the kind of impact his words would have on readers of all ages. He certainly did not know how long it would be before he saw his name in print again. It's a good thing Spinelli dared to believe that he could be paid to be a writer. It was a dream he had to keep believing in for the next 25 years.

Spinelli (left) as a member of the Phi Gamma Delta fraternity at Gettysburg College. He was the fraternity historian.

Failing Like
a Champ

COLLEGE LIFE

After high school, Spinelli decided to stay close to home. He enrolled at nearby Gettysburg College, where he majored in English. We do not know if his grades had returned to his usual A's. We do know that he joined many clubs, much like he had done in middle school. He made good use of his love of sports and writing to become the editor of the *Gettysburgian*, the school newspaper. According to the college's Web site, the *Gettysburgian* is "a student newspaper of Gettysburg College, providing news, features, sports, arts, and opinions relating to the campus community."[1] In 1961, Spinelli's sophomore year, he was editor of the *Mercury*, the college's literary magazine. With only a few chances each year to have students' work published in the magazine, it may have been quite a thrill when Spinelli entered their fiction contest with a story called "Growing Up" and won.

It's not surprising that the young man who was voted most popular boy in middle school would find it easy to fit into a fraternity in college. He served as a member of the Interfraternity Council and the Registration Committee, and he also joined Phi Gamma Delta. He became that fraternity's historian.

Not much is known about Spinelli's college years, but in *Night of the Whale,* the main character, Mouse, feels that he is not ready for college. He is supposed to go to college to study journalism, but he does not think he can because the only thing he knows about is drinking beer. Perhaps Spinelli was remembering his college and fraternity life. He may have found that he and Mouse had a lot in common as college-bound young men. In the Gettysburg College archives, there is a copy of an unpublished short story, "Vandy's Star," that Spinelli wrote. It was "inspired by fraternity Christmas houseparties."[2]

When Spinelli graduated from Gettysburg in 1963, he had an A.B. (Artium Baccalaureatus). This degree is awarded to students who study liberal arts, such as English literature. In 1992, Spinelli's college presented him with the Distinguished Alumni Award. The award is given annually to graduates for their "professional and/or civic accomplishments post-Gettysburg."[3]

After Gettysburg, Spinelli moved on to Johns Hopkins University in Baltimore, Maryland, for his postgraduate degree. The classes and workload require that students "produce a substantial manuscript in the form of a novel or collection of fiction or poetry"[4] prior to graduation. While attending seminars, Spinelli wrote a story called "Old Men," which was published in *Charles St. Review* in 1964. This manuscript may have fulfilled his requirement for graduation. During the writing seminars, Spinelli had been given the tools he needed to be a good writer. When he graduated in 1964, he expected that his life as a published author was soon to come. He was mistaken.

THE RESERVE

With two degrees, Spinelli was well trained academically for life as a writer, but there was one thing that he still needed to do. "Every passing day, every February 1—the date of my birth—prodded me closer to the ominous cloud that hung over my future. It was called the draft, and it meant that when I (and all other boys deemed healthy enough) got out of high school or college, I would have to join the armed forces whether I wanted to or not."[5] In 1965, Spinelli felt that he had put off facing his fate long enough. Rather than wait to be drafted, he decided to enlist in the Naval Air Reserve. It allowed him to do his duty to his country while still pursuing the writing life. Even while in training at Lowry Air Force Base in Denver, Colorado, Spinelli found time to write. The Gettysburg College archives have a story called "The Egg Trick" that he wrote during his time there.

Spinelli served in the Naval Air Reserve until 1972. He was required to serve one weekend a month plus two weeks in a row every year. With the military requirement out of the way, he now had one less thing on his mind, but because he still was not making money as a published writer and reserve duty did not pay much, he had to find a regular job.

TWO YEARS THAT BECAME 23

His first job was teaching composition to college students at Temple University in Philadelphia, Pennsylvania. He left after just one semester because he felt that the job required too much thinking. In 1966, he found employment at the Chilton Company in Radnor, Pennsylvania. First, he worked as an editor of *Department Store Economist* in the winter and spring of 1966. It still wasn't what he was looking for. He switched to become an editor at *Product Design and Development*, a trade magazine for engineers. "That was exactly the kind of place I wanted to work when I got out of college. I wanted a job that was boring, that would not challenge me, so I could spend the rest of my time writing."[6] When he got on the job, Spinelli says, "I told the secretary I was writing a book so I would only be there for a year or two. That turned into 23."[7]

In fact, Spinelli took every spare moment he possibly could to do his writing. He had a small, windowless office on the fifth floor. At lunchtime, he shut his door to write. He wrote more at night and on weekends, even on the weekends he was serving in the Navy Reserve. During those years, what he wrote went mostly unpublished and largely unrecognized. His first four novels, *Song of Rosalie*, *The Life of Joe Francis Pigg*, *The Shoe*, and *The Corn Goddess*, were written for adults. Spinelli said that he was trying to get them published, but "nobody wanted them."[8] He even wrote a three-act play called *The Revolution of Jane Rice*, as well as a screenplay for Disney. His only small success came with the publication of a short story titled "Letter from Cape May." It was printed in *Buffalo Spree Magazine*, a small regional magazine published in Buffalo, New York. He wrote the story in 1967, but it was not published in *Buffalo Spree Magazine* until 1975.

In the many years that Spinelli worked at Chilton, he kept sending out his work to potential publishers. All of it was rejected. What does a writer do when many letters from publishers come in the mail with a resounding "no"? "You just keep plugging on," Spinelli told a group of young readers in Illinois in 2003. "I felt like putting my head in an oven every time I got a rejection slip. But you'd get the rejection slip on Monday, and incredibly you wake up Tuesday, and you're still alive. Wednesday, you feel not that great but not as rotten as you did on Monday."[9] Spinelli always picked himself up and submitted the manuscript to another publisher.

Although they might take up to six months to review a writer's manuscript, most publishers do not like it if writers submit their work to more than one publishing house at a time. This is called "multiple submissions." Would-be authors can wait six months to get a rejection letter and then must send it to another publisher and wait six more months for a response, either positive or negative. As a result, sometimes years can go by before a manuscript is accepted.

The many years of rejection were frustrating for Spinelli. In that time, though, he was doing work that would help him be a great writer later on. He thought of what he was doing as "writing practice," just like a pianist might do scales before a big performance. While at Chilton, Spinelli began to write notes that would later become *Stargirl*.

The notes for the novel *Stargirl* had begun even before Spinelli encountered a woman named Eileen Mesi, but Spinelli believes that Eileen was more like Stargirl Caraway than anyone he had ever met. Spinelli and Eileen both worked at Chilton, but they did not know each other for a while. Spinelli first became aware of Eileen when he found a chocolate bunny on his desk at Easter. Eileen had put it there—she had given everyone a chocolate bunny. Spinelli still didn't know who she was until they bumped into each other one day while waiting for the trolley.

"Eileen had—as she always did in those days—three or four loose-leaf binders stuffed with her poetry, and she shoved them into my arms and made me read them while we waited for the train. For some reason she was impressed that I was an editor at the magazine where we both worked."[10] Once the two of them realized that they were both struggling writers, they became friends.

On May 21, 1977, Spinelli married Eileen Mesi and became stepfather to her six children. Despite the pressures of having a family to care for, the Spinellis continued to pursue their dreams of becoming published writers. The continuous flow of rejection letters did not stop them. Spinelli believes that it is important for kids to understand that everything in life is not about success. "Have any of you kids ever heard a speech on failure?" he asked a group of fans in Indiana. "No, but you sure hear about success. Failure is much more common than success."[11] Spinelli feels that failure is just as important, perhaps even more important, than success. "Failure is not potholes, but stepping stones," he said. "Sometimes you have to do the goofiest thing of all, the craziest thing—start over."[12] In a 1996 interview, Eileen agreed that it is often hard to keep on writing after so many rejections, but she said that they didn't get defeated and stop. They believed that they were good writers and that they should keep trying. In an interview, Spinelli remarked,

Did you know...

Besides his wife, Eileen, Spinelli's favorite writer is Loren Eiseley, who was known for his essays and poems. He died in 1977.

"You do it because you want to do it. You make the time because you want to . . . and you're willing to let some other things go."[13] Fortunately, when the rejections kept coming in, the Spinellis had each other for support. Although the couple had good jobs at Chilton, they were not making a lot of money and they had to let go of a few of the comforts of everyday life. "I wrote for fourteen years without a dime to show for it," Spinelli said. "If it were just the two of us, we could've lived on beans in an apartment. For years, that's how we survived—on thrift shops, yard sales and double coupons." Fortunately, as Eileen has said, "I love thrift shops and yard sales anyway."[14]

With a half-dozen kids in the house, it was often difficult to get any writing done, but the Spinellis made house rules that allowed them to work. One was, "No kids allowed on the first floor after 9:30pm, even if you're in high school."[15] Spinelli admits that he tried nearly everything to create a good environment to write in. "I even wrote away for a gizmo that makes ocean sounds to cover background noise but there's no surf that's a match for six kids in the house," he said. Eileen found writing in the middle of the night much easier and often stayed up "until two in the morning writing."[16]

Eileen wanted to be a poet. One of her favorite authors was Edna St. Vincent Millay, a popular American poet who died in 1950. Eileen's success came, though, when she began to write for children. Today, she writes picture books for very young kids. "Picture books are a lot like doing a poem," she told an interviewer. "The focus is narrow and there's a definite shape to the words."[17]

Spinelli had a wife who understood the writing life, and the ground rules they had set for the house helped him do his writing. He seemed well on his way to achieving his goal; however, it did not happen quite the way he had expected. It happened quite by accident.

A photo of Ray Lincoln, Spinelli's longtime literary agent, who died in 2008. Lincoln was a champion of unpublished writers, including Spinelli, whose work she pushed to have published.

4

The Lost Lunch

CHICKEN BONES

If you are a fan of Jerry Spinelli's work, you have probably already heard the famous chicken bones story. If you have not, it happened something like this: In the 1980s, when money was tight, Spinelli used to take his lunch to work in a paper bag to save money and precious lunchtime writing minutes. One night, the Spinellis had chicken for dinner and he put the leftovers in a bag. When he went into the refrigerator to get the bag of chicken, he found only a bag of bones. One of his six children, who were now asleep in their rooms, had eaten the fried chicken in the middle of the night and put the bones back in the refrigerator. He went to work, but the idea of the bag of bones would not leave him. Just like on the night of the football game in high school, Spinelli sat down and wrote about the incident. As usual, the experience was not quite over in his mind until he put pen to paper. "Little did I know, I was beginning my fifth book,"[1] he told a reporter years later.

First, he thought about writing the story from the point of view of the adult who had found the bag of bones. Then he thought it might be funnier from a different perspective—the chicken-eating kid's perspective. "I found a bag of bones in the refrigerator—and an idea for a book. It was an idea that bit me. There was no procedure. It just happened, and I began writing. There was no expectation."[2] Just as when he was in high school, he did not know then that what he was writing, just a reaction to an experience, was going to be publishable material. "I started writing about fried chicken," he told a group of nearly a thousand fans in 2003. "Suddenly my life changed. I had just started writing my first published book."[3]

The chicken bones incident is something Spinelli calls "muse visitation." [4] The muses were nine goddesses from Greek mythology whose job was to inspire artists such as poets and painters, and in Spinelli's case, even children's book writers. This particular visit from a muse helped to spark the novel that Spinelli titled *Stuff.* The chicken eater became seventh grader Jason Herkimer. Spinelli wondered, though, if Jason's story would have the same fate as his first four novels. Since college, he had been writing steadily every moment he got, and all four of his manuscripts had been sent to publishing houses and agents, and they were all rejected. "However, because it was about a thirteen-year-old boy, adult book publishers didn't even want to see it,"[5] Spinelli recalled. He might have been facing down another rejected novel, but he found an agent just in time.

HAIR

A local author recommended agent Ray Lincoln to Spinelli, and he mailed the first three chapters of the incomplete novel to her. Lincoln informed him that she only reviewed finished manuscripts. The story might have ended there, except that Eileen Spinelli called her and somehow got Lincoln to make an exception to her usual rules for reviewing a new author's work. "Eileen was driving the horse of my bandwagon for a long time," Spinelli said in a *Publishers Weekly* piece,[6] meaning that Eileen was his biggest fan, fiercest advocate, and, obviously, his most convincing ally. "The most thrilling moment for me, in publishing, was not the publication of my first book or any other," he said. "It was the letter I got from Ray Lincoln on a Saturday morning, telling me that she really liked my work."[7] Until she

Did you know...

According to the Society of Children's Book Writers and Illustrators, new writers can expect to be paid only up to $8,000 per book for young adult novels. If the book sells well, they can earn royalties, or a percentage of the sale price. A 10 percent royalty will give a writer $1.50 for every $15 book sold. Go to http://www.scbwi.com for more information.

retired, Ray Lincoln remained Spinelli's agent, and he still has that very first letter of acceptance. (Lincoln passed away in 2008.)

With an agent on his side, it was time to send out the novel to publishers. John Keller, who worked for Little, Brown, describes how he first encountered the manuscript:

> I first came upon Jerry's work sometime in 1981 when a manuscript by a writer I'd never heard of from an agent I didn't know landed on my desk. The title was promising enough: *Space Ship Seventh Grade*. The subsequent decision to change it to *Space Station Seventh Grade* (Little) occupies several ongoing chapters in the Spinelli-Keller correspondence that might be called "I see what you're trying to tell me, but. . . ." When I began to read, I liked the first chapter's conversational, unpretentious tone. It wasn't, however, until I got to the fourth chapter, "Hair," that I knew I had happened upon a writer who was special. When I read that chapter, in which Jason Herkimer tells about his ambivalent feelings about the onset of puberty and the absence or presence of pubic hair as noted in the boys' shower room after gym class, I broke into a big grin and thought, Exactly![8]

Keller believed that Spinelli had deftly expressed what every 13-year old boy felt in locker rooms all over the country. "That, I believe, is Jerry's greatest strength. He gets it right. He gets the details right."[9] Keller gave Spinelli a contract, and in 1982 *Space Station Seventh Grade* was published. Spinelli was 41. It had taken 25 years to fulfill his dream of becoming a published author, and it was in children's literature, a genre he had never even considered. Said Spinelli, "That's how, by accident, I became an author of books for kids. Life is full of happy accidents."[10]

THE LIBRARY

Jason Herkimer and Spinelli had a lot in common. In fact, Jason's experiences mirror Spinelli's boyhood quite accurately. In one chapter, Jason describes how he feels about school. The reader can almost hear the young Spinelli saying the same thing about his experiences in the tenth grade. "The first week of school is over. I hated it. I'm not going back. I wish I was back in the sixth grade. I was important there. I'm nothing here."[11] When Jason thinks about the satellite *Pioneer* drifting out into space, it gives him goose bumps. That could very easily have been the young Spinelli on his solitary walks through Norristown.

Spinelli wrote *Space Station Seventh Grade* in the first person because he felt that the character "Jason Herkimer had been only too happy to tell his own story,"[12] but it seems as though Jason was merely a conduit for Spinelli's own feelings. In an interview with The Author Corner in 2000, he says that, of all his characters, "I relate to [Jason] the most."[13] Spinelli put his novel and his feelings on the line when the book was published. Now all that was left was waiting for the critics' reviews and to see if there were any readers interested in this particular seventh-grade boy. When the reviews finally came in, there were good and bad.

Kirkus Reviews called Jason "macho" with "some ridiculous racial misconceptions" and considered the book "funny," not "as frivolous as it seems at first; but . . . consistently zippy and bright."[14] Most readers, however, became ardent fans of the book, so much so that, 24 years after first being published, *Space Station Seventh Grade* is still being reprinted. It has been printed twice in hardcover, three times in paperback, and once as a special edition for libraries. Many readers felt that Jason's story should be required reading for anyone heading to high school. To respond to his fans, and because it seemed that the Jason story could continue, Spinelli published a sequel, *Jason and Marceline*, four years later.

Spinelli himself mused on why *Space Station Seventh Grade* and Jason Herkimer hit home with kids. In a 1994 interview, he was asked if he gets his ideas from remembering the recent past or his life long ago. "Long ago," Spinelli replied.

> I've gotten letters from kids, for example, telling me how much they enjoyed *Space Station Seventh Grade*, which was my first book, and telling me how it's just like it is with them in seventh grade. And I think there's something very telling there, because my reference point for *Space Station Seventh Grade* was not these kids who are writing to me in 1993, but it was in 1953 when I was in seventh grade. It tells you that basically kids don't change.[15]

In another interview, Spinelli described kids' letters that ask "How do you know so much about me?" He thinks it's funny that some people think that he must "hide in closets and record conversations." He does not, of course. "I draw on my memories. Kids are still the same. They have different problems, but still, fundamentally, they are the same."[16] *Space Station Seventh Grade* remains Spinelli's favorite book because it was the first one he had published. It might also be because Jason is so much like himself as a young man.

With the publication of this book, Spinelli was on his way. He was now an author. He had an agent, and he had fulfilled a dream 25 years in the making. The money he made off of *Space Station Seventh Grade* was not nearly enough to maintain a house full of kids, though, and Spinelli would have to spend a few more years writing during his lunch hour and at night after the kids went to bed before he could make the job of "writer" his full-time day job.

Above, Jerry Spinelli reading Who Put That Hair in My Toothbrush?, *with young fans, in 1987.*

5

A Writer at Last

THEY WOULDN'T SHUT UP

Spinelli had hit pay dirt with a 13-year-old protagonist. He was able to use the experiences from his own childhood to write a story that was worth publishing and that got good reviews from critics and fans, and he loved the idea of using his memories as a resource. In the book *Speaking for Ourselves,* Spinelli described why the adventures he had as a boy are perfect adventures for his characters:

> Each of us, in our kidhood, was a Huckleberry Finn, drifting on a current that seemed tortuously slow at times, poling for the shore to check out every slightest glimmer in the trees . . . the taste of

45

Brussels sprouts ... your first forward roll ... cruising a mall without a parent ... overnighting it ... making your own grilled cheese sandwich ... the weird way you felt when Sally Duffy scrunched next to you in the mob coming out of the movie ... the thousand landfalls of our adolescence. And the current flows faster and faster, adulthood's delta looms, and one day we look to get our bearings and find that we are out to sea.

And now we know what we did not know then: what an adventure it was![1]

Should he have gone back to writing for and about adults? Spinelli feels that his stories are for everyone. Although his main characters are young adults, there are plenty of adults in his stories. "I let my stories find their own audience and hope that the result is a story readable by adults and kids."[2] Even now, Spinelli does not like to pigeonhole himself as a "children's author." "In my own mind, I really don't write for kids," he said. "I write about kids."[3]

Spinelli followed up *Space Station Seventh Grade* with a story he called *Siblings*. It was inspired by the constant bickering of two of his own kids, Molly and Jeffrey. Keller, his editor for *Space Station*, liked the story but insisted on changing the title, which he thought was too boring. Together, they came up with a new title: *Who Put That Hair in My Toothbrush?*

In this story, 12-year-old Megin (Megamouth) and 14-year-old Greg (El Grosso) are siblings who do nothing but argue. Spinelli wrote the story from both of their points of view by alternating the speaker in each chapter. He told both of their sides of the story because "it had been all I could do to shut them up."[4] The book is fast-paced, moving from one incident to another as the siblings continue to one-up each other's destructive behavior. For example, Megin destroys Greg's science project, and Greg retaliates by throwing her hockey stick into a pond. Besides being each other's worst enemy, the two have other problems. Greg has a crush on a girl who has moved away, and Megin despises a new girl in school. When a crisis happens, though, the brother and sister finally band together. A reviewer for *Children's Literature* wrote how "the book accurately depicts adolescent travails and the fierce battles that often erupt within otherwise loving families."[5]

In 1988, the book was nominated for the Indian Paintbrush Book Award, which is presented to the author of the book that receives the most votes from children in Wyoming. Fans of the book found it hysterical despite, or perhaps because of, crude scenes such as the vomit in the cider vat. *Toothbrush* was reprinted three times in paperback and released as an audio recording in 1998. It was reprinted as a hardcover as late as April 2000. In 1984, an Italian-language version of the book was also released.

THE WORST REVIEWS EVER

Although Spinelli had found success with younger main characters, he was still used to writing about adults. With *Night of the Whale,* Spinelli's third novel, he went in between, writing about a boy just graduating from high school. The story is set at a family resort in Ocean City, New Jersey. Mouse, the main character, shares a beach house with his former school newspaper colleagues the week after high school graduation. The story centers on these teens growing up in the face of a difficult problem—what to do about a group of whales that have beached themselves on the shore. The immature Mouse suddenly grows up when he tries to figure out how to help the whales, if they can be helped at all. *School Library Journal* called the book a "seemingly interminable string of descriptions of beer guzzling followed by flatulence, beer guzzling followed by vomiting, beer guzzling followed by urinating contests and beer guzzling followed by hangovers. . . . Many teens won't stay around until day five of this hedonistic week . . . those who do will have a hard time buying it."[6] Many other reviews were just as painfully negative. *Night of the Whale* was released in paperback three years after its first release. It has never been reprinted. Perhaps Spinelli listened to his critics because he never produced a story with an older main character again.

SEQUEL

A year later, in 1986, Spinelli returned to familiar ground with the main character of his first novel. Jason Herkimer was back, and this time, he had a girlfriend, Marceline. Once again using the memories his younger self, Spinelli remembered how he felt when he tried to figure out exactly where he stood with the women in his life. Just as he struggled with the idea of how to be respected and how to be a man, Jason in the story thinks that he needs to hit somebody to get respect. The scene is similar to an incident from Spinelli's youth. On the way home from school one day, he decided to hit one of his friends. "I balled my fist and swung, and . . . my knuckles landed—thock—against his chin bone,"[7] Spinelli recalled.

The simply titled *Jason and Marceline* was an opportunity for Spinelli to regain his footing on familiar ground. Perhaps Spinelli the adult writer was not so different from the young man, as he sought out approval and the title of "good boy" or, in this case, "good author." He got it. The reviews for *Jason and Marceline* were considerably better than the ones he received for *Night of the Whale*.

Publisher's Weekly called the sequel "fresh and funny, sometimes crude, sometimes poignant, and always very real."[8] A reviewer from *Children's Literature* called the book "decidedly raunchier" than other books for teens and said that it was about "humor and heartbreak up against hormones."[9] *School Library Journal* reviewer Robert Unsworth noted that Jason's "X-rated mind has to cope with a girl who thinks kissing is quite enough for now" while his friends are "scoring." Later in the review, Unsworth wrote, "Spinelli can be very funny, if very crude. Some adults will shudder or sputter over this one, but YAs will love it. It's a quick, witty read, and even the print is big."[10]

Jason and Marceline was reissued in hardcover and paperback as recently as April 2000. It had been reprinted in paperback twice before that, in 1988 and again in 1994. In 1986, the book was translated into German.

Did you know...

Spinelli is a member of the Chester County Astronomical Society and the American Fancy Rat and Mouse Association. He included his pet rat, Bernadette, in *There's a Girl in My Hammerlock*. Another pet rat appeared in *Stargirl*.

Spinelli lunching with students in 1990, the year he published The Bathwater Gang *and* Maniac Magee. *Although popular with young adult readers in the previous decade, during the 1990s Spinelli would reach a new level of success.*

SUMMER STORIES

In Spinelli's next two books, he left school behind and dealt with the problem every kid has and loves to have on the last day of school: what to do over summer vacation. In 1988's *Dump Days,* best friends J.D. and Duke are determined to have one perfect day before the summer ends. This involves zeppoli eating, playing video games, buying comics, and bike riding in front of trucks. Unfortunately their chosen activities require money, and they don't have the necessary funds, so they create schemes to earn it. A reviewer for *Publishers Weekly* wrote, "Spinelli spins a story that weaves together the shared conversations and small-town adventures of a friendship based on trust, humor, compassion and imagination."[11] Readers immersed in the story can see the reflections Spinelli must have had from his own small-town life as he told J.D. and Duke's story. *Dump Days* also deals with racism directed at a young Vietnamese violinist—a theme that Spinelli would explore at length again in his most famous and critically acclaimed novel. Although it received good reviews, *Dump Days* was reprinted only once in paperback and is currently out of print.

For *The Bathwater Gang,* published in 1990, Spinelli told the story of J.D. and Duke's younger sisters. This was written for his youngest audience yet: Critics put the age range between grades one and three. Bertie Kidd (J.D.'s sister) is bored one summer, and, at her grandmother's suggestion, she decides to start a gang. The only rule is that no boys are allowed. Unfortunately, only one girl joins (Duke's sister), and the neighborhood boys don't like it, so they form a gang of their own. This sets off a summer filled with rivalry, ending in a mud fight that brings the whole group together. The title comes from the girl gang's summer business—a mobile pet-washing service. *School Library Journal* found the story "light [and] entertaining."[12] *The Bathwater*

Gang was released twice in paperback in 1992 and again in 2005.

The 1980s were a good decade for the Spinellis. Eileen's first book, *The Giggle and Cry Book*, was published in December 1981, and Jerry was publishing his novels steadily. Although their books were selling, children's authors typically do not make a lot of money, and it was especially hard for the Spinellis to make ends meet with six children in the house. Nevertheless, Spinelli decided to leave his editorial job at Chilton in 1989, the year before *Bathwater* hit the shelves. He may not have felt very certain about leaving a secure job, but it turned out to be a very good move. In a 1996 interview, he recalled how "nobody ever told me how hard it was going to be to make a living as a writer,"[13] although it seems as though his editor John Keller may have warned him. After Spinelli won the Newbery Medal, Keller wrote an article about him. In it he describes when Spinelli told him about leaving Chilton:

> Then he told me that he was quitting the job and was going to spend all his time writing novels! Any editor who hears that news and does not shake in his boots for the author must have a heart of stone. We all know how difficult this business is for novelists who write for young people. They strive; they struggle; and, even when they succeed, the monetary rewards are usually less than generous. I think I said something about how tough such a life might be, but Jerry told me that he had thought about it long and hard and that he wanted to give it a try. What could I say? Let me put it this way: I thought he'd be back at the technical publisher before long.[14]

For Spinelli and his readers, his risk was worth it. His career was just warming up and his best writing was yet to come.

Above, a page of Spinelli's notes for Maniac Magee, _his novel that won the Newbery Medal in 1991._

6

Maniac Mania

PATCHING THE QUILT

First, there was a boy running "3 miles to the hoagie shop, 6 miles to the nearest movie theatre."[1] This was the image that had come to mind when he began work on his next novel. This time, however, Spinelli was borrowing from someone else's experience. A friend of Spinelli's had done all that running, a boy who had lived in a Catholic orphanage from the time he was nine months old. When the boy was seven or eight, the kids from the orphanage were taken to a swimming pool, but Spinelli's friend was not admitted because he was black. Until Spinelli had heard of this, he had not known that being black made a difference. The idea of his friend being turned away from the swimming pool at such a young age and the fact that he began to run everywhere after that incident, got stuck in Spinelli's head. (Spinelli himself had done a fair amount of running in his youth, along the train tracks near his Norristown home.) "I tucked it away, in that little pretty-bug drawer we writers all have, along with the dozens, hundreds of other appealing tidbits awaiting the right setting, the right story."[2]

The right story began to form itself while Spinelli was still working at Chilton. He had finished *The Bathwater Gang* and began to make notes for his next novel. "I asked myself: Now what do I feel like writing? The answer: I feel like writing a book about a hero, a kid who's a hero especially to other kids. I think kids want to be heroes. I think that in many small, often unacknowledged ways they are heroes. I wanted to write about that."[3] He tried to pin this idea of a hero to a location. The character had to have a house, or a school, just like all his previous characters, but this character didn't seem to fit in any of those places. He kept waiting and looking out for the right pieces to put together. Along the way, he read about a kid nicknamed Maniac in a column that appeared in the *Philadelphia Inquirer.* He liked the name. "I thought it fit the character,"[4] he told The Author Corner. Then he borrowed the last name from a childhood friend, Dennis Magee.

Maniac first appears in *Dump Days* like a dot on the horizon. One character describes him as "an orphan sort of kid, who sleeps at the bandshell." The idea of a kid sleeping out in the open seemed strange to Spinelli, so he decided to ask some other people what they thought.

He called a friend who was a schoolteacher and he tried to explain the character, a boy who never goes to school, lives in a buffalo pen at the zoo, and has no family. His friend was not sure that such a character would work. He decided to ask someone else. His editor, John Keller, was much more encouraging when he called and asked, "John, can I write a book about a kid who doesn't have a family or a home and doesn't go to school?" His editor "scarcely hesitated," Spinelli said, and told him "sure."[5] He was on his way.

Although the character had been on Spinelli's mind for a long time, in a 2000 interview with Jennifer Brown, he said it was hard for him to write the book. It took a few tries to start Maniac's story. What happened was what Spinelli called his "second documented muse visitation."[6] He had left work frustrated, unable to find the right words for the story, but when he got home, something happened. "I was in my office one night doing something else, and that's when the words came to me: "They say Maniac Magee was born in a dump." Spinelli said, "I've never had the sense that I reached down and took hold of that sentence. It simply came to me."[7]

The words "they say" at the beginning of the story set the tone for a story about a larger-than-life hero, a myth, a legend. The story itself did not disappoint. Spinelli reached from far and wide to create the world that readers enter in *Maniac Magee.* The setting is his familiar Pennsylvania; some places take on new names, and others remain intact. The Schuylkill River is there, as is the bridge that leads to Bridgeport, Maniac's birthplace. The real DeKalb Street is the dividing line between the east and west end of Norristown, and this became Hector Street in Maniac's story. Marshall Street, where Spinelli lived in one of the row houses, became Sycamore Street, where Amanda Beale and her family live.

The people of *Maniac Magee* come from everywhere, too. There is a scene in which Mrs. Beale puts her finger in Maniac's mouth, just as Dr. Winters put his finger in then three-year-old Spinelli's mouth. There is the "black sixth-grade girl [he] had met in a school somewhere in New York's Ichabod Crane country." A teacher told him that this girl had a strange habit. "Every day she carried her entire home library to school in a suitcase, lest her beloved books fall to the crayons and teeth of her siblings and pets at home."[8] He left his contact information with the girl and asked her to write to him, but she never did. She probably does not know that she inspired the character Amanda Beale. Then there is Grayson, a major league player, teaching Maniac about baseball. He mirrors Spinelli's coach Skat Cottman, who threw what he called the "stop ball." "It comes up to the plate all big and fat," Spinelli recalled. "Then it stops and waits for you to swing, and then it goes on to the catcher's mitt."[9] The pitch was almost impossible to hit, perhaps a little like Grayson pitching to Maniac. Maybe it was also a little bit like the frog ball that was hit in a lot, a lot very much like the one Spinelli played in as a boy.

Every minute detail of the story comes from a scrap of Spinelli's life. Near the beginning of the story, Maniac carries Amanda's book all over town. Spinelli admits, "I regret that I did not read and write more as a kid. That's why I have Maniac Magee carrying a book in his hand as he's running along the tracks or going to play baseball.

It's as though I'm kicking it the second time around, and this time, doggone it, I'm going to do it right."[10] All of these scraps of memory came together to form, as Spinelli wrote, "a patchwork quilt: the sources and elements of a novel stitched together to form a blanket that is at once varied and coherent."[11] The quilt work took up so much area that it required three boxes to hold all the *Maniac Magee* notes and drafts in Gettysburg College's archives.

Even with all these details to use, Maniac's story would not focus on one issue. The essential story problem was not there. "It was great for Maniac, I suppose," Spinelli said, "but terrible for the book."[12] He decided to take the opportunity to address the issue of racism, which he had been thinking about for some time. He reached into his old notes and took out the only chapter of a book he had titled *The Race*, in which the town's two fastest kids, one white and the other black, race against each other.

Once the novel was published, the critics' reviews were mixed. A *Publishers Weekly* reviewer called it a "modern-day tall tale" and an "off-the-wall yarn [that] will give readers of all colors plenty of food for thought."[13] A critic for *School Library Journal*, however, wrote, "Warning: this interesting book is a mythical story about racism. . . . It's a cop-out for Spinelli to have framed this story as a legend—it frees him from having to make it real."[14] Spinelli's fans, though, loved "that Maniac" without reservation. They were not the only ones.

THE FACTS MIXED UP WITH THE TRUTH

Mary Blandin Bauer was appointed to the Newbery committee in 1989. The Newbery Medal is named for John

Newbery, an eighteenth-century English bookseller, and has been awarded annually "to the author of the most distinguished contribution to American literature for children"[15] since 1922, according to the American Library Association's Web site. In 1990, Bauer read nearly every piece of children's literature that was published. She and the other committee members compiled lists of nominees and sent them out to the other members, and she discussed several titles with reading groups and fellow librarians. Among the nominees for the award were *The True Confessions of Charlotte Doyle* by Avi, *Libby on Wednesday* by Zilpha Keatley Snyder, and *Other Bells for Us to Ring* by Robert Cormier.

The voting began in October. On January 10, 1991, "recognized authorities in children's literature and some former Newbery Award committee members discussed three titles—*The True Confessions of Charlotte Doyle, Libby on Wednesday* and *Maniac Magee.*"[16] The decision

Did you know...

The ISBN number is a series of numbers on the bar code of every book that is used to identify and track books. R.R. Bowker is the company that controls ISBN distribution in the United States They recorded that approximately 175,000 books were published in 2003. In 2004, 195,000 books were published.

had to be made by January 14, and a press conference was scheduled despite the fact that the winner had not been chosen. The committee came together, and each person had the opportunity to describe what was important about each book. Then it was time to vote. According to Bauer, "The Newbery balloting is unique, and precisely dictated. The winner must have a margin of eight votes over the next title and must have at least eight first-place votes. For each ballot each member votes for a first, second and third choice, with four votes for first, three for second and two for third."[17]

At the end of the night, the winner was *Maniac Magee.* The committee had been impressed with Maniac, who they called a "superhero." The runner-up was Avi's *Charlotte.* Once the voting was over, the committee's job was nearly done. All that was left to do was make one phone call.

THE INFERNAL RINGING

The phone rang at 12:30 A.M. Spinelli recalled in his Newbery acceptance speech that he "was doing what all respectable Pennsylvanians were doing at 12:30 A.M., a half-hour after midnight: I was sleeping." He ran to stop the "infernal phone from ringing in the middle of the night."[18] Since he and Eileen were the parents of six kids, they feared that a midnight phone call was most likely bad news. Eileen assumed it was, since she thought she heard him say the word "metal" instead of "medal." Instead, they got the best news a young adult author can get: Spinelli found out that *Maniac Magee* had won the Newbery Medal. The honor of the phone call had gone to Alice Naylor. The first thing she said was, "We want you to know that we have been very careful not to let the facts get mixed up with the truth."[19] It was a reference to the opening passage of *Maniac Magee.* "Is this a joke?"[20] Spinelli asked. She informed him that it was not.

The Spinellis celebrated until dawn and then went out for breakfast—French toast and bacon. When they returned, they finally got some sleep, and then the phone started ringing again. This time, it was the rest of the world, having just heard the news, calling to get interviews and to give congratulations.

On June 30, 1991, Spinelli delivered his Newbery acceptance speech in Atlanta, Georgia. He thanked the committee, his editor, the copy editor, the cover designer, and the photographer who had taken a picture of a boy's running feet for the first edition of *Maniac Magee.* His main thanks, though, were for the kids, his readers. Spinelli described Maniac Magee as "both the kid we all once were and the kids we now look after. He is us and ours, was and is. And insofar as he has no address, everywhere is his home; insofar as he belongs to no one, everyone is free to claim him."[21]

Ten years after *Maniac Magee*'s first publication, Spinelli said that he would recommend it as the one book of his that should be read "for the message, the story and the language."[22] He has also said that Amanda Beale is one of his favorite characters. Obviously, readers the world over feel the same way. Not only did *Maniac Magee* become the Newbery Medal winner in 1991, it also won the Boston Globe–Horn Book Award in 1990, the Notable Children's Books Award (from the American Library Association) in 1991, and the Best Books for Young Adults Award (also from the ALA) in 1991. In addition to the Newbery Medal, the book has won 20 other awards in children's literature, the earliest in 1990 and the latest in

1996. *Maniac Magee* has been translated into Japanese, Portuguese, and Korean. It was made into an audio book and a Nickelodeon movie.

Although now a critically acclaimed and popular author, Jerry Spinelli would find himself reaching even greater heights of success in the coming years by branching out into new areas of fiction.

Jerry with his favorite pet rat, Bernie, in 2000. He included his pet rat in There's a Girl in My Hammerlock. *Another pet rat appeared in* Stargirl.

7

Other Books

FUNNIER STUFF

After Spinelli created the legendary Maniac Magee, he returned to more realistic characters. He still wanted to address important issues, though, and in his next novel he took a look at gender bias. A year before the publication of *There's a Girl in My Hammerlock,* Spinelli read a newspaper article about a girl who joined her high school wrestling team. In a photo accompanying the article, the girl was shown on the scales in the weight room. He said, "Once again, I felt slapped in the face with an idea."[1]

Eighth-grader Maisie Potter is one of the best athletes in school. She joins the wrestling team to get closer to Eric, the boy she likes. This makes her the only girl on the team, and both her teammates and her friends are upset about it. The reviews for Spinelli's latest novel were mixed. Although Maisie's "trials and triumphs make for a highly satisfying tale" in a story that was "clever, witty and tightly written," the reviewer for *Library Journal* felt that Spinelli didn't "break any new ground."[2] Calling Maisie a "female Maniac Magee with an intact, nurturing family," a reviewer for *School Library Journal* noted that "kids will eat [the story] up."[3]

There's a Girl in My Hammerlock was first published in 1991 and was reissued as a hardcover as recently as 2002. In 1993, the book won the California Young Reader Medal. In 1994, it won the Charlotte Award.

There's a Girl in My Hammerlock was published by Silver Burdett Press. It was the first book Spinelli had worked on with a publisher other than Little, Brown. Spinelli moved on to another publisher after this one, as well: He got a contract to do a four-book series called School Daze for Scholastic. The contract must have been a great relief to the Spinelli family: Although Spinelli was making a living as a writer, he still was not making a lot of money, and a four-book series meant a steady paycheck.

The first in the series, *Report to the Principal's Office,* was published in 1991. The main character, Eddie Mott, is a good boy like Spinelli was and is given the honor of raising the school flag up the flagpole. Calling it "a chuckle a chapter," Pamela K. Bomboy declared in *School Library Journal* that Spinelli's latest book was written with "sparkle, humor and warmth."[4] Unlike in some of his previous books, there are no heavy social issues in *Report to the Principal's*

Office, just a group of middle school students trying to adjust to the first weeks of school.

In a 1999 interview, Spinelli said that, when he began to write his next book, he relied on a memory from his grade school days. "I remembered the chant: 'Fourth Grade Rats.' The title came first, and I had no idea where to go with it. I sat down and worked up a story to go along with the title."[5] The playground chant that inspired the title went like this: First grade babies! Second grade cats! Third grade angels! Fourth grade rats!

With *Fourth Grade Rats,* Spinelli returned to a story with a message. The message this time was about peer pressure. Joey and Suds are friends, but Joey takes the school chant too seriously. He thinks that becoming a man is all about being tough. Suds does not want to be a "rat," but he allows Joey to pressure him into rebellious behavior. *Publishers Weekly* applauded Spinelli's "rapid-fire dialogue and [the] hilarious string of episodes." *School Library Journal* called some of the characters "exaggerated but believable" and thought that some of the "scenes in which Joey tries to toughen up Suds [were] especially funny."[6]

Fourth Grade Rats, first published in 1991, was reprinted 2003. In 1993, the book was given the South Carolina Children's Book Award. In 1995, it earned the Black-Eyed Susan Award.

In 1992, Spinelli returned to his original publisher, Little, Brown. He also returned to the *Dump Days* and *The Bathwater Gang* characters. The result was the sequel *The Bathwater Gang Gets Down to Business.* In his book *Jerry Spinelli,* David Seidman asked why Spinelli wrote sequels. Spinelli said that he usually does not like to do it: "Generally, I don't like to write or read sequels. They're seldom as good as the originals."[7] Spinelli had already done a sequel with *Jason and Marceline*, however, and he would again. One fan once asked if he would ever do a sequel to *Maniac Magee*. He said he would not.

In *The Bathwater Gang Gets Down to Business*, the gang's pet-washing service is not finding any customers and they need money for circus tickets. Bertie thinks up a dishonest plan to create business: She starts to dirty pets herself. Her grandmother comes to the rescue again and puts a stop to her behavior. *Booklist* called the story a "sunny, lightweight chapter book" that is "perfect for the age group."[8]

Also in 1992, two books in the School Daze series, *Who Ran My Underwear Up the Flagpole?* and *Do the Funky Pickle*, were released by Scholastic. In *Flagpole,* the four main characters get involved with football, one of Spinelli's favorite sports. Sunny becomes a cheerleader, Eddie tries out for the football team to impress her, Salem becomes team manager, and Pickle takes the lead on the marching band. In *Do the Funky Pickle,* the story of these four friends continues. Pickle tries to teach Eddie how to dance so that Sunny will like him. By the time *Picklemania*, the final book in the School Daze series, was released in 1993, all four characters were involved in romances.

In the three years since he had left his full-time job at Chilton, Spinelli had worked tirelessly at his writing. Eight of his books were published, and with the awards and praise that his books were receiving, Spinelli was also making a name for himself, not just among readers, but among teachers, librarians, and publishers too.

TOOTER TALES

For *Tooter Pepperday,* a novel published in 1995, Spinelli used incidents from his own life for the story details.

Nine-year old Tooter's father quits his day job to become a writer, and the family needs to save money. As a result, they have to move away from Tooter's beloved suburbs and all of her friends. The Spinellis did not move to a farm after Spinelli left Chilton, but they certainly understood the need to save money. Also like Spinelli, Tooter's father becomes so absorbed in his work that he barely notices anything or anyone around him while writing. One day, to get his attention, Spinelli's daughter Molly wrote a note going up the margin of his notepad. "I could show you a piece of yellow paper from one of my published books. You'd notice handwriting of another style going up the margin."[9] Just as he did with the chicken bones incident, Spinelli changed the perspective to tell it from the kid's point of view. When it appeared in the book, it looked like this:

> Tooter found her father at his computer. . . .
>   She coughed to get his attention. He kept pecking. When Mr. Pepperday was writing, he forgot the rest of the world.
>   She sat on the keyboard.
>   He noticed.[10]

A reviewer from *Children's Literature* called it "a delightful beginning chapter book for emerging readers."[11] *Booklist* said that the story has "enough farm jokes and silly scenes to keep readers turning the pages."[12] A reviewer from *School Library Journal* reported that "Tooter Pepperday . . . is sure to bring on the chuckles and the giggles."[13]

Because Spinelli was not fond of repeating characters, he probably would have moved on from Tooter at the end of the book, but he agreed to do a second one: "The second Tooter Pepperday book, *Blue Ribbon Blues,* was the publisher's suggestion . . . as I recall."[14]

Blue Ribbon Blues was published in 1998, three years after the original. It is about Tooter trying to adjust to living on the farm. In this sequel, her aunt prompts her to enter a goat in a blue-ribbon contest at the county fair. She also has to deal with her brother, who wants to paint the goat, and a coyote that threatens all the blue ribbon contestants. Like the original, this Tooter tale met with great praise. *School Library Journal* called the writing "light, fast-paced and humorous."[15] *The Horn Book* called Tooter "a real-life, plucky, resourceful heroine."[16]

THE OUTSIDERS

The books written in these years were funnier than much of Spinelli's earlier work, but they did not receive the kind of critical praise that had been given to *Maniac Magee*. For his next book, *Crash*, Spinelli decided to tackle a more serious subject. Set in Pennsylvania, the story allowed him to highlight another sport: the Penn Relays, an annual series of track and field events that began in 1895.

One of the novel's characters, Penn Webb, is named after the Penn Relays by his great-grandfather. The main character is Crash Coogan, an athlete and bully. At the start of the book, he mistreats Penn, a Quaker and vegetarian, because he enjoys picking on kids who are different. After a tragedy in his life shows him how alike he and Penn are, they wind up becoming good friends. Once again, Spinelli used perspective to his advantage. One critic observed in *Publishers Weekly* that "Spinelli takes the brawny, bullying jock who is the villain in so many middle grade novels and casts him as the narrator of this agile tale. . . . [W]ithout being preachy, Spinelli packs a powerful moral wallop, leaving it to the pitch-perfect narration to drive home his point [about bullying]."[17] A reviewer from *Children's Literature* was also

From left, Louisiana State's Kelly-Ann Baptiste, Juanita Broaddus, Samantha Henry, and Brooklynn Morris pose for a team photo after winning the college women's 4x100 championship at the Penn Relays in April 2008. The Penn Relays, an annual series of track and field events that began in 1895, plays a central role in Spinelli's novel Crash.

impressed that the story was told from the point of view of the "antihero who's a bully-jock."[18] Connie Tyrell Burns noted in *School Library Journal* that "readers will devour this humorous glimpse at what jocks are made of while learning that life does not require crashing helmet-headed through it."[19] In addition to receiving almost universal praise, *Crash* received 14 different awards.

Spinelli followed this success with *The Library Card*. This book contains four stories with one common item: a library card that changes the life of each character. The idea for this book came from his editor at Scholastic. Each tale focuses on a character that a reader might not like at first, and Spinelli told their stories with his usual humor, attention to character, and plotting. The first character, Mongoose, is a shoplifter. He finds the card mixed in with a stash of stolen candy. The next is Brenda, who is addicted to television. The Great TV Turn-Off sends her to the library looking for a story. In a strange twist, she finds a story about herself—something that is far more interesting than anything she ever watched on the tube. The third character is Sonsaray. He is an angry teen, but he begins to enjoy children's story hour. The final character, April Mendez, moves to the country, far away from the great libraries of the city, but she finds a bookmobile that takes her on a strange ride.

A critic for *School Library Journal* loved Spinelli's "unique characters and lively wit,"[20] and a reviewer for *Children's Literature* said that the stories "touch both the heart and the funny bone."[21] *Publishers Weekly*'s reviewer, however, in addition to believing the stories to be "vaguely unsettling," felt that the idea of a library card that somehow makes everyone's life better was "contrived"[22]—meaning that the idea seemed forced and unnatural.

In Spinelli's next book, *Wringer*, a 9-year-old boy dreads turning 10 because, after that birthday he will have to become a wringer. During the town's annual pigeon shoot, he will have to find pigeons that are wounded and kill them by wringing their necks. Spinelli's fear of the draft inspired the fears of the book's main character, Palmer LaRue. Like Palmer, he did not want to face his fate: Spinelli did not want to fight in a war, just as Palmer did not want to kill wounded birds.

When Palmer turns nine, he joins a popular gang. He needs to be tough to fit in with the guys in the gang, so he hides the fact that he does not want to be a wringer because he is afraid that his new friends will call him a sissy. He is also hiding a pet pigeon named Nipper in his bedroom. A critic for *School Library Journal* said that Palmer's problem is "a moral dilemma familiar to everyone: How does one stand up for one's beliefs when they will be very unpopular?"[23] At the end of the story, Palmer finally does have to stand up for himself. *Children's Literature*'s reviewer thought it a "welcome relief"[24] for the reader. A critic for *Kirkus Reviews* noted how Palmer's "inner battle between revulsion and his desire to fit in" is heavy reading, but it has "some belly laughs from Spinelli to lighten the load."[25] Benjamin Cheever, in his review for the *New York Times*, noted how Spinelli presented the problem "with great care and sensitivity" and said that "Jerry Spinelli is not a bore."[26]

Wringer received a Best Books citation from *School Library Journal* in 1997. It was a Newbery Honor Book and won the Carolyn W. Field Award and the Josette Frank Award in 1998.

Spinelli has always used his childhood as research to write his books. For his next book, he decided to steer away from fiction and write a memoir of his youth. In 1998, *Knots in My Yo-Yo String: The Autobiography of a Kid* was published. The book documents Spinelli's life up to age 16, beginning with his grandfather, Alex, and ending when Spinelli decided to become a writer.

While Spinelli worked on this book, he changed how he worked. He had previously written his books longhand on notepads. When he began *Knots,* he started using the computer. He was also working on two books at once. He told an online group how "at one point I was writing both *Knots in My Yo-Yo String* and *The Library Card* at the same time." In another interview, he explained that he was "writing one on the computer in the morning and [the other] by longhand in the afternoon."[27]

A reviewer for *Publishers Weekly* felt that, when "Spinelli effortlessly spins the story of an ordinary Pennsylvania boy, he also documents the evolution of an exceptional author."[28] The story was a series of ordinary events, but as a *Children's Literature* critic noted, "the telling makes all the difference."[29] In *The Horn Book*, Peter Sieruta remarked that Spinelli's "intense awareness, and thoughtful observations were all signs of his eventual career."[30]

As a new millennium dawned in 2000, *Stargirl*—a book that would launch Spinelli's career to greater heights—was published. The main character, Stargirl Caraway, is the kind of girl who cheers for anything and who makes any day a celebration. Stargirl is an almost mythical character, much like Maniac Magee had been. This character's exuberance may seem to have been inspired by the start of the millennium, but Spinelli had in fact started working on her story while he was still working at Chilton. At that time,

Did you know...

Stargirl gift cards were made for Barnes and Noble booksellers and offered to buyers starting in 2006.

he tried to write a story about a boy who lived in the sewers, but it was going nowhere. In that original story, which Spinelli wanted to call *Under the Bomb*, Stargirl's name was Moonshadow. He wanted to write a character that was "emulatable," which means that her behavior could be easily adopted, "and not beyond the reach of today's kid, as someone who is larger-than-life might be."[31]

In the published novel, Stargirl Caraway joins the cheerleading squad and cheers even when the other team scores. Fellow classmate Leo Borlock does not know what to think of her at first, although at the beginning of the story no one else minds Stargirl's odd behavior. Reporting for *Teacher Magazine,* Stephen Del Vecchio described why Stargirl has a hard time:

> It seems Stargirl can't restrain herself from cheering regardless of which team scores. Initially, no one minds much because, for the first time in memory, the Mica Electrons basketball team looks like it may go undefeated and reach the state playoffs. The school soon becomes obsessed with winning, and when the Electrons lose a crucial game, Stargirl's cheers for the opponent's shots are blamed. Almost overnight she goes from being revered to despised and ignored.[32]

When the rest of the school turns on her and her odd ways, they pressure Leo to do the same.

Spinelli began to write the notes for *Stargirl* before he met his wife, but he later recognized much of Eileen in the character. He told Jennifer Brown, "If there was any model for Stargirl at all, it would be Eileen."[33] He has said that, if anyone would cheer for the other team, it would be his wife.

Critics heaped praise on the novel. A reviewer for *Publishers Weekly* called Stargirl "part fairy godmother, part outcast, part dream-come-true."[34] An *ALAN Review* critic called it "another well-written work by Spinelli that will particularly appeal to young people and their eagerness to discuss today's high school culture."[35] Spinelli's fans were just as impressed with the book, believing that it teaches people to accept themselves and others no matter what their differences may be. In addition to being popular in the United States, *Stargirl* was published overseas in Finnish, Portuguese, Korean, and Arabic.

With *Stargirl,* Spinelli found his niche as a writer and moved away from lighter stories like *Tooter Pepperday* and *The Bathwater Gang.* His newer stories often focus on older characters who are dealing with somewhat more controversial issues. In an interview for The Author Corner, he talked about why there are some similarities in his books, including the theme of acceptance: "I deliberately strike a similar note from story to story, hopefully with some variation, like a fugue. In other cases, it just happens. There is bound to be some story-to-story similarity in an author's body of work. My goal is originality of recipe, not ingredients."[36]

In *Loser*, published in 2002, the character Donald Zinkoff is similar to Stargirl Caraway. Just like Stargirl, fourth-grader Donald sticks out in a crowd, and, like many of Spinelli's other characters, his lack of interest in "regular" behavior lands him in trouble. Even when his classmates tease him, he barely notices it. He is always happy and positive about everything, including school. On field day, Donald causes his team to lose an important match, and his classmates brand him a loser. From this point on, he realizes his classmates have always thought he was an oddball. He is hurt and upset, but after he has a few experiences with people outside of his school, Donald begins to believe in himself again and gets back some of his positive attitude. In the end, everyone sees that, although Donald is odd, he is a person to be valued. They all realize that every person needs to be seen for who he or she is on the inside.

A critic for *Book Magazine* called the novel a "compelling character study [that] may inspire readers to reevaluate how they judge their fellow students and whether winning matters more than caring does."[37] *Publishers Weekly* gave the book a starred review, which meant that the reviewer considered the novel to be outstanding. A reviewer for VOYA (*Voice of Youth Advocates*) wrote that "the author uses Zinkoff to show readers another definition of the word hero."[38]

BREAKING NEW GROUND

In 2003, Spinelli tried his hand at something new: a picture book. Eileen may have had a lot of input on this story because she had been working on them for years. The result of Spinelli's effort was *My Daddy and Me*, a tale about a pup and his daddy who do all kinds of fun things when the father comes home from work. The pup gets to ride on his father's shoulders, and they pretend drive to Kalamazoo. They make cookies and plant tomatoes. The story ends as most tales for young children do, with a lullaby after the pup has been tucked into bed. A reviewer for *Publishers Weekly* said that "the scenarios may not be new, but the warmth emanating from parent and child is comfortingly universal."[39] *Children's Literature*'s reviewer called the book a "joyful celebration."[40] A critic for *Kirkus Reviews* described how "the intensity and directness of feeling will strike a chord in young readers."[41]

Also in 2003, *Milkweed*, a very different Spinelli book, was published. Spinelli set the story during World War II in Nazi-occupied Warsaw, Poland. Once again, he chose to tell this compelling tale through the eyes of an orphan. Like Maniac Magee, Misha seems to have sprung up out of nowhere and gets by on his own. Misha does not know his name, and he has no family. He does not know his history, and he barely understands what is going on around him. Misha tells his story without emotion, even when he describes the terrible things that happened during that time. He does not know what the Nazi soldiers with their shiny tall boots really do or that the parade of singing orphans heading to the trains is a frightening, tragic scene.

In an interview published in *Scholastic Scope*, Spinelli said that he was inspired to write the story because of a childhood memory. "It goes back to when I was a little kid paging through a history book of my father's. Pictures of the concentration camps prompted an interest and a caring that's been with me ever since." He also said that he called the book *Milkweed* because "the milkweed puffs, rising from their pods and floating into the sunny sky contrast with the grim setting. They suggest hope and better times."[42] Spinelli said that he wrote the story "because there is no statute of limitations on humanity. Because history sits on the shoulder while story unlocks the heart. Because to those involved, there was not a Holocaust of six million, but six million Holocausts of one."[43]

The ALAN Review's reviewer wrote, "*Milkweed* is heartbreaking, not only for its honest look at an abhorrent series of events, but also for its realistic portrayal of the toll these events take on a boy, his adopted family, and his misfit friends. The book successfully captures these people in all their frail humanity, their joy and follies, their triumphs and tragedies."[44] In addition to receiving good reviews, *Milkweed* also won the Golden Kite Award in 2003. In 2004, it was selected as an American Library Association Best

Book for Young Adults and was a National Jewish Book Award finalist.

After *Milkweed*, Spinelli did not publish another novel for several years. When he finally returned to publishing in 2007, he published not one but two books. In the first book, *Eggs*, Spinelli described the friendship between 9-year-old David and 13-year-old Primrose. David has just moved to Minnesota to live with his grandmother after his mother died in a freak accident. Primose spends most of her time in an abandoned van to get the space she needs but does not have in the one-bedroom apartment she shares with her mother. After they meet, David and Primrose forge a bond that helps them recover from their sorrows. Spinelli's other book that year, *Love, Stargirl*, was a sequel to the first Stargirl book. It takes place a year after the first book and is written as a letter penned by Stargirl to her ex-boyfriend, Leo. Spinelli's most recent novel is *Smiles to Go*, which was published in 2008.

In a 1996 interview with Diana Winarski, Eileen Spinelli said that she and her husband "could never write together. I don't understand how people do that."[45] In my interview with Jerry Spinelli, however, he revealed that he and his wife are in fact collaborating on a nonfiction book.

A recent photo of Jerry and Eileen Spinelli. The husband-and-wife authors have spent their careers inspiring and supporting each other's work.

8

How He Does It

TIME TO WRITE

With more than two-dozen books, several articles, and numerous awards under his belt, Spinelli has a measure of luxury that comes with being a well-known children's book author. This means that he can relax a little, knowing that the time he has is his own to create stories. At the beginning of his career, this was not the case. In the early years, the kind of perseverance that his editor admired while Spinelli was still working at Chilton served him well. He powered through 14 well-received books in 11 years with the pace of a gale-force wind. How did he do it?

The first problem that any writer faces is finding enough time to write. In the early days, there were six kids in the house. Today, there are 16 grandkids occupying the Spinellis' time. In a 2005 interview, Eileen discussed what she called "writing in the crack" of the day's busy schedule:

> It can be tricky because there are only so many hours in a day. We have a big family—16 grandkids so far. So family comes first and happily so. Next comes writing time. I keep in mind that what I wanted to be when I grew up was a writer, not a speaker. It can be fun giving talks . . . and it's always delightful to meet readers, but if I said "yes" to every invitation, I'd never write a word. A writer also needs chunks of totally unstructured time—time to think, to dream, to meander. That time has to be woven in, too! Not to mention the laundry![1]

For the same reasons, Spinelli admitted, "I'm not traveling on author tours or for book reasons as much as I used to."[2] Spinelli's scheduled writing time includes working for a couple of hours in the morning in his home office on the second floor and then again at night. The Spinellis moved from their previous home, where Eileen used to work in their garage, which they had turned into a writing cottage. Now, they both have offices on the second floor. This makes it even easier for them to look over each other's work. Spinelli calls their new home a "two-office, one-bedroom house."[3] He says that his office is his favorite place to work.

Even with more time and great success, Spinelli still finds the job of writing to be a daunting task. In a 1996 interview, he admitted, "It's seldom a day when I feel like writing. Nine out of 10 days there's a resistance to overcome . . . but it's part of the territory. Writing doesn't do itself. One way or another, I get down to it and get something done." Eileen agreed. "You have to have some structure," she said in the same interview. "There has to be a balance of freedom and responsibility."[4] Despite his resistance to start working, Spinelli says that "I aim to write every day."[5] Eileen explained that "we talk about our writing every day at lunch, we read chapters of each other's work and bounce ideas off one another."[6]

Jerry Spinelli has relied on Eileen as a sounding board for his work. In his Newbery acceptance speech, he thanked her. "My wife and fellow author, Eileen, who says yes or no to every chapter, whose judgment I trust more than my own, and who creates the world in which I write. When the committee gave the award to me, they gave it to us."[7] Their writing relationship is mutual. "I feed Eileen my books chapter by chapter. If they're not right, she tells me so. If they are, she acts as a cheerleader. And I try to do the same for her."[8]

WHY WRITE?

Spinelli has discussed how the act of writing down a story or a poem completes the event in his mind. Separate from

> ### *Did you know...*
>
> **When Spinelli works, he likes to stay comfortable in jeans, a pair of moccasins, and a flannel shirt. He might also drink water or orange juice.**

this need to see something through to completion is the need to communicate. Spinelli believes that this need is not inherent just in writers, but in all of us. When he visits schools, he asks the students:

> "Why do you write?" I say, "If you're coming to school on the bus in the morning and as you're zooming by Tenth Street you see on the corner one of the most incredible things you've ever seen, what are you going to do as soon as you get to school?"
>
> Everybody's hand goes up. They knew the answer. "I'm going to tell my friends."
>
> That's it. There's a natural urge in everyone to communicate experiences that they have, whether those experiences are something you observe, something tragic, happy, poignant, sad, unusual, or incredible. You want to tell somebody about it. It's hard to keep it to yourself. When I think of myself as writing today, you could say that what I'm doing in effect is continuing this telling.[9]

Spinelli's goal is not just to entertain the reader, but to enter into a partnership with the reader to create a story. "A book is a collaboration, a joint project, between writer and reader," he explained when he was asked to participate in a citywide reading campaign for teens in Philadelphia. "With every hand that turns to the front page, with every pair of eyes that begins to read the first sentence, a book is born anew. A writer's most honored mission is not only to reach and touch a reader, but to encourage him or her to become a reader in the first place."[10] This collaboration is what keeps his fans connected with his writing despite the passages of time and distance. *Space Station Seventh Grade* still appeals to new readers nearly 20 years after its first publication. A fan in Illinois said that Spinelli's writing "relates to lots of people."[11] Indeed it does. His novels continue to be translated into different languages as readers from every corner of the globe find that his characters speak directly to them.

Spinelli's other goal is to use his words to affect his reader exactly the way he needs to for the story. This process of finding the precise words to suit the speaker and to describe the scene is the difficult task of writing. "In my opinion the hardest part of writing a book—sometimes—is getting onto the page and into the reader the same picture and feeling that I have inside me."[12] This is where Spinelli reveals his skill.

THE RIGHT WORDS

Spinelli has said time and time again "write what you care about. If you do that, you stand the best chance of doing your best writing." In almost every interview, he says the same thing when asked to give advice. It is what he calls a "golden rule"[13] for writers. "It seems to me, from the reading and writing I have done, that the writer who writes what he or she cares about—if the writer writes well—touches a reader."[14] Also, he said, "Beyond that, I try to give a sense of the totality and the variety and richness of a life well lived."[15] This means that he concentrates on the details that make a book more vivid.

Fans and critics alike have praised Spinelli for his ability to always write the right words. "You can hear the people's voices very well,"[16] said sixth-grader Diane Latino in 2003, at a Spinelli signing and reading at Anderson's Bookshop in Illinois.

This ability comes through hard work. Most of the time, Spinelli does not know what to write next. He once told an online group that, if a camera was watching him work, "it would show me sitting in front of this computer with a blank look on my face wondering what the heck to write next." Later on, he was asked to "complete this sentence. As a writer, I am like a ___ because ___." He said that he is "like a horsefly because I bounce from idea to idea."[17] Spinelli keeps track of all of those ideas by writing them down as soon as he gets them. He says there are about 250 ballpoint pens around his house. As soon as an idea comes to him, wherever he is, he writes it down.

Because ideas can come from anywhere and can happen at anytime, Spinelli advises writers that the best thing to do is "stay alert, because ideas do not come through the same door every time. Close your eyes and see what bites you. The main thing is to be alert and pay attention."[18]

Where does Spinelli get all these good ideas? "It's easy to get ideas, but not easy to get good ideas,"[19] he said in an interview for The Author Corner. In his interview with David Seidman, he went even further: "Great ideas are a special, rare thing. But good ideas, frankly, are a dime a dozen. Often the critical factor is not in recognizing a good idea when you see one but in executing it into a good story."[20]

Spinelli does not always rely on his childhood memories for material. Sometimes his sources have to come from outside and that requires diligent research. For *Wringer,* he did not know much about pigeons or pigeon-shooting. To get the details right, he recalled, "I spoke with friends who keep pigeons. And I read an interesting book about someone in England who had one."[21]

A combination of memories, writing what he cares about, research, and hard work are the ingredients that go into Spinelli's books. Which of those does Spinelli think is the most important ingredient? A student once asked him what he would include in a "Writing Kit." The first item he mentioned was "a head full of memories."[22]

THE TECHNICAL STUFF

"Before I write," Spinelli has said, "I regularly read *Walking on Alligators: A Book of Meditations for Writers* by Susan Shaughnessy."[23] Then he reads the previous day's work out loud. He believes "it's a good idea to stop while you're still cooking because it's easier to pick things up the next day."[24] Then he gets to writing. It often takes him "from one month to one year [depending] on the book"[25] to finish a story. In that month or year, he is making up stories "on a day-by-day, chapter-by-chapter, page-by-page basis." He says that he is "not good at foreseeing moments in my stories until I'm almost there."[26]

Are there any tricks to writing well? Spinelli is not sure. He admits that, although he enjoyed sentence diagramming when he was in school, he does not think that "the fact that I could analyze a sentence had [anything] to do with the fact that I could write a good sentence."[27] Unlike many students, he found exercises such as identifying parts of speech and spelling fun and enjoyable. "I was good at little mechanical detail, analysis type things like that. That's not to say that it had anything to do at all with making me a writer. It was just a game for me."[28]

A fan once asked if Spinelli had a set number of metaphors and similes that he used as he wrote. "I write them as they seem appropriate. I make them up,"[29] he said. In an interview, Raymond P. Kettel asked if he makes them up after he is finished with a passage and then goes back in to apply them. Spinelli replied:

> It's not as deliberate as that. It has to do with trying to communicate. It has to do with trying to make as vivid and effective a picture of what you're trying to say. It's abstract in your head, and I never forget that what I'm trying to do is make a connection with the reader. It doesn't mean a thing if it doesn't connect, if it doesn't communicate. I'm not writing to myself; I'm writing to the reader. I'm building a bridge to the reader; I'm trying to touch the reader. So metaphors and similes are ways of highlighting and projecting what I see out there, so the reader can see what I'm seeing in my head; it's clarification.[30]

Spinelli does not do a lot of rewriting. He learned to work efficiently during those lunchtime writing sessions at Chilton. He also does not let the technical stuff like checking punctuation and spelling stop him if he is on a roll. He thinks that if writers are onto a good idea, they should keep going and worry about the spelling and punctuation later. He does give one caution, though: Writers "need to strike a balance between spontaneity and deliberation. If you work too fast and spontaneously, then you could wind up with a mess."[31]

The one thing he would like to share with writing teachers is that they should allow their students a chance to write freely and let their ideas take them wherever they might lead. He believes that if students have a set format to follow, they do not get the opportunity to be creative. He thinks that it is better to have a guideline, and then teachers should let students "freewheel," or write whatever they like: "When a student has an opportunity to freewheel, that's when you're going to discover the real gems."[32]

Paul Feig, the creator of the TV series Freaks and Geeks *and the author of two memoirs, will write and direct the film adaptation of Spinelli's* Stargirl, *which is due to be released in 2009.*

Beyond Books

GOING HOLLYWOOD

One day at an author visit in Indiana, Spinelli read a letter from a fan. She loved *Maniac Magee* and suggested that Spinelli contact Steven Spielberg to see if he would make the book into a movie. Spinelli said that Spielberg was not interested but Nickelodeon, a division of Disney, was.

It is impossible to pass a movie theater these days without seeing the name of a children's book on the marquee. Perhaps it was inevitable that Spinelli would be approached to make one of his books into a movie, but would it be a movie that really reflected the book? Spinelli maintains a wait-and-see attitude toward all film adaptations of his work. "Most movies fall short. I'll be pleasantly surprised if this is an exception. I still prefer the film that rolls in the reader's head."[1] Elijah Wood, who played Frodo in *The Lord of the Rings* trilogy, bought the rights to *Maniac Magee* because he had hoped to play the title character. Instead, the role went to Mike Angarano, who had played a part in a previous Nickelodeon movie, *Say Uncle.* The cast also included Kyla Pratt, of *One on One* and *The Proud Family* fame, in the role of Amanda Beale. Jada Pinkett Smith was cast as Mrs. Beale. Although they were all experienced actors, Spinelli did not think the final film, which was released in 2003, was a great adaptation of his book. He said that he would have done it differently if he had the opportunity to work on it himself.

Spinelli has made movie deals for four of his books, including *Maniac Magee.* At that time, the *Maniac Magee* movie had not aired and *Stargirl, Crash*, and *Wringer* were not being worked on yet. Recently, the rights to *Milkweed* were bought. In 2004, Paul Feig, the creator of the series *Freaks and Geeks*, discussed how he signed on to write and direct the film adaptation of *Stargirl.* He told a reporter for *Variety*: "I fell in love with the theme of what happens if you meet your soul mate in

Did you know...

Paul Feig, who signed on to direct the *Stargirl* movie, is an author himself. He has written two memoirs. The first is called *Kick Me: Adventures in Adolescence*. The sequel is called *Superstud: Or How I Became a 24-Year-Old Virgin.*

high school, before you are ready, and it runs smack into the rules of teen popularity and acceptance."[2]

STARGIRL SOCIETY

In her freshman year of high school, Michelle Luscre hung out with her friends in the drama club and no one else. It was a clique like thousands of others in middle and high schools the world over. "I wouldn't have been able to stand us," Michelle said. "The backstabbing and things that went on were ridiculous." Then she read *Stargirl,* and she and her friends wanted to change their critical ways. They wanted to find a way to be themselves and to celebrate their differences. She also wanted to reach out to younger girls. Maybe she could change the negative experience of cliques for them. What she and her friends started to talk about in their freshman year became known as a "Stargirl Society." They got 24 seventh- and eighth-grade girls at her middle school to join. The goal was to guide these 24 middle school girls to be themselves and lead them to a positive experience in high school. The girls began by talking about how to accept themselves. Then they read and discussed the book and sent Valentines with personal messages to every student. They even brought in "Starwomen" from the community, women who would talk to the girls and inspire them. As a final event, the girls stayed overnight at the high school. They played games and had a talent show and an "inner-beauty" pageant. Michelle and the other high school girls talked to the middle school kids about what they could expect in high school. The group's efforts were successful.

In March 2006, Spinelli and his wife visited the school to attend a Stargirl Society meeting. In June, Michelle and the other founders received first prize from the Future Problem Solving Program International. They have shared

Above, a meeting of a Stargirl Society. Inspired by Stargirl's open-mindedness, the society's founders wanted to find a way to be themselves and yet celebrate their differences. Since that time, chapters have popped up across the country—and in countries like New Zealand and Canada. Jerry Spinelli's Web site now offers information about how to establish your own Stargirl Society branch.

information about the Stargirl Society with schools in New York, Georgia, Texas, California, and Pennsylvania, and there are international Stargirl Societies in New Zealand, Australia, and Canada.

Spinelli has updated his site with information on how to create a Stargirl society, as well as activities, such as how to create a Stargirl bookmark.

BACK TO SCHOOL

In 1992, Gettysburg College honored Spinelli as a Distinguished Alumnus. They later acquired his entire body of work—all of his manuscripts, notes, and copies of his published and unpublished works as well as media adaptations—and now have these items in the archives at the college. In 2000, Spinelli was awarded an honorary Doctor of Literature degree by Western Maryland College. In 2006, Gettysburg College senior Julia Grover put Spinelli's *Stargirl* notes and manuscripts on display for the Special Collections and College Archives. The exhibit was titled *Stargirl: The Writer's Craft—Manuscripts from the Jerry Spinelli Papers.*

THE FUTURE

What's next for Spinelli? With a nonfiction book in the works and movies waiting to be made, we certainly have not seen the last from this remarkable writer. It seems that we might be hearing from one of the Spinellis' children soon, as well. On Eileen Spinelli's Web site, she mentions that several of their children like to write poetry and that one of their sons has an idea for a novel. It is not surprising that the Spinellis have inspired their own children to write. The two show how the challenges of the writing life can be worth it

Spinelli thinks that a writing career is great. He says that becoming a writer turned out to be "the best career of all, because in telling my stories I can be all those things I ever did and did not become."[3]

Despite his success, Spinelli balks at the idea of being called a writer. "I'm beginning to wonder if I ever really became a writer," he says on the Web site Kids Reads.

> I find that I hesitate to put that label on myself, to define myself by what I do for a living. After all, I also pick berries and touch ponies and skim flat stones over water and marvel at the stars and breathe deeply and grin from ear to ear and save the best part for last. I've always done these things. Which is to say, I never had to become anything. Or anyone. I always, already, was. Call me a berry-picking, pony-touching star-marveler.[4]

APPENDIX

An Interview with Jerry Spinelli

TRACEY BAPTISTE: Your college Web site lists you as George E. Spinelli, is that correct? What's the "E" for?

JERRY SPINELLI: George Elwood is on my birth certificate. As the story goes, my Aunt Margaret saw me shortly after birth and said, "He doesn't look like a George. Call him Jerry." And it stuck.

TRACEY BAPTISTE: Who advised you that your first novel should be submitted to children's publishers?

JERRY SPINELLI: Nobody. No one wanted my first four novels. By number five I had an agent, who submitted the manuscripts to adult departments, who told her this is a book about a kid, adults won't read it. So she turned to juvenile editors and that's where *Space Station Seventh Grade* landed, with Little, Brown.

TRACEY BAPTISTE: Once you found success in children's literature with *Space Station Seventh Grade,* did you ever think about writing another book with an adult main character?

JERRY SPINELLI: Yes. I think about it less and less, as I do include characters of all ages in my stories.

TRACEY BAPTISTE: Did winning the Newbery for *Maniac Magee* change your approach to writing books? For example, do you feel more pressure? Less?

JERRY SPINELLI: Only in that I had less time and more distractions. I had to learn to close the door on all the fuss, stick cotton in my ears and get back to work, remind myself that I'm a writer, not a visiting celebrity.

TRACEY BAPTISTE: Do you still get rejection slips from publishers?

JERRY SPINELLI: Now I sign contracts before I write the books.

TRACEY BAPTISTE: What did you think of the movie *Maniac Magee*?

JERRY SPINELLI: I wasn't crazy about the movie. I would have done it differently. Other books, including *Stargirl*, are under option. I've had a little more input with them and am hoping they turn out better if they ever reach the big screen.

TRACEY BAPTISTE: How do you work on manuscripts? I've read that you write longhand first.

JERRY SPINELLI: I work on the computer now. It took me a while to change from longhand to computer, and at one time I was writing one book in the morning longhand and another at night on the computer. Now it's almost all computer unless I'm writing on the train.

TRACEY BAPTISTE: How does Mrs. Spinelli help you as you write?

JERRY SPINELLI: Eileen passes judgment on each chapter as I finish it. She's my first editor. I seldom oppose her views.

TRACEY BAPTISTE: Might you and Mrs. Spinelli ever write a book together?

JERRY SPINELLI: We're doing one now. Nonfiction.

TRACEY BAPTISTE: What is your wife's favorite book of yours?

JERRY SPINELLI: *Space Station Seventh Grade*.

TRACEY BAPTISTE: Have you always come up with the titles for your books?

JERRY SPINELLI: Except for the first two. My title for the first one was *Stuff*. Editor didn't like it, said give me more. I gave him 22 more. He didn't like any of them. So he titled it himself: *Space Station Seventh Grade*. I wish I had stuck with *Stuff*. Second one I called *Siblings*. Boring, said my editor, rightly. She suggested *Who Put That Hair in My Toothbrush?* and that was that. I guess I've gotten a little better title-wise since then.

TRACEY BAPTISTE: How do you know when the title is right?

JERRY SPINELLI: It just seems to fit, like a shirt. Sometimes it's the first thing to come, sometimes the last. I didn't title *Stargirl* till halfway through the writing.

TRACEY BAPTISTE: Gettysburg College has archives of a lot of your writing, including your first attempt at a novel, *Song of Rosalie*. Why did you keep those manuscripts for such a long time?

JERRY SPINELLI: More than anything, I guess it was simply sentiment. And a sense that if no one else was ever going to possess my stories, at least I would.

TRACEY BAPTISTE: Which of your books was the most difficult to write?

JERRY SPINELLI: Each is difficult in its own way. None stands out. I would say *Knots in My Yo-Yo String* was the least difficult. It's my autobio, so the "plot" was already there; I didn't have to make it up.

TRACEY BAPTISTE: I noticed on your site that *Stargirl* is now published in Arabic. Why do you think that so many children from such diverse backgrounds can connect with your books?

JERRY SPINELLI: People are people—everywhere.

TRACEY BAPTISTE: When did you feel secure enough with your writing career to consider becoming a full-time writer?

JERRY SPINELLI: Never. I simply didn't want to go to my grave never having tried. I doubt that any writer is totally "secure," no matter the level of success.

TRACEY BAPTISTE: What do you think makes a good writer?

JERRY SPINELLI: Caring what you write about. Details of character and place.

TRACEY BAPTISTE: There are already two Jerry Spinelli biographies published. Besides the one I'm working on now, there is another that was published in March 2007. How does it feel to know that so many people want to know about you?

JERRY SPINELLI: It's flattering. The best part is that it implies my books have readers.

TRACEY BAPTISTE: What would you most like people to know about you and your writing?

JERRY SPINELLI: That I found myself with a few years on this third planet from a midsize star and I used stories as a way to reach out and touch my fellow creatures.

TRACEY BAPTISTE: What is the best part about being a children's book author?

JERRY SPINELLI: Honestly, I don't label myself that way. I simply think of myself as a writer. I like to think I write for everyone.

TRACEY BAPTISTE: What is your favorite thing that a fan ever asked or told you?

JERRY SPINELLI: "You make my world glow."

CHRONOLOGY

1936   Spinelli's parents, Louis Spinelli and Lorna Bigler, are married.

1941   George Elwood ("Jerry") Spinelli is born.

1945   Spinelli's brother, Bill, is born.

1946   Spinelli moves to the west end of Norristown, Pennsylvania, and enters first grade at Hartranft Elementary.

1955   Enters tenth grade at Norristown High School.

1957   Moves to Locust Street in the north end of town; "Goal to Go" is published in the newspaper.

1963   Graduates from Gettysburg College with a bachelor's degree in English.

1964   Receives his Master of Arts degree from Johns Hopkins University.

1965–1974   Serves in the United States Naval Air Reserve.

1966–1989   Edits technical magazines for the Chilton Company.

1969   Completes his first novel, *Song of Rosalie*, which is never published.

1977   Spinelli and Eileen Mesi are married.

1982   Little, Brown publishes his first book under the title *Space Station Seventh Grade*.

1984   Little, Brown publishes *Who Put That Hair in My Toothbrush?*

1985   Little, Brown publishes *Night of the Whale*.

1986   Little, Brown publishes *Jason and Marceline*.

1988   Little, Brown publishes *Dump Days*.

1990   Little, Brown publishes *The Bathwater Gang* and *Maniac Magee*.

1991   *Maniac Magee* wins the Newbery Medal; Scholastic publishes *Fourth Grade Rats*; Simon & Schuster publishes *There's a Girl in My Hammerlock* and *Report to the Principal's Office.*

1992 Little, Brown publishes *The Bathwater Gang Gets Down to Business*; Scholastic publishes *Who Ran My Underwear Up the Flagpole?* and *Do the Funky Pickle.*

1993 Scholastic publishes *Picklemania.*

1995 Random House publishes *Tooter Pepperday.*

1996 Random House publishes *Crash.*

1997 Scholastic publishes *The Library Card*; HarperCollins publishes *Wringer.*

1998 Random House publishes *Blue Ribbon Blues: A Tooter Tale*; Alfred A. Knopf publishes *Knots in My Yo-Yo String: The Autobiography of a Kid*; *Wringer* becomes a Newbery Honor Book.

2000 Alfred A. Knopf publishes *Stargirl*; Spinelli is awarded an honorary doctorate from Western Maryland College.

2002 HarperCollins publishes *Loser.*

2003 Alfred A. Knopf publishes *My Daddy and Me*; Random House publishes *Milkweed*, which wins the Golden Kite Award; Gettysburg College honors Spinelli as a Distinguished Alumnus.

2006 Spinelli and his wife reportedly start to work on a nonfiction book.

2007 Little, Brown publishes *Eggs*; Alfred A. Knopf publishes *Love, Stargirl.*

2008 HarperCollins publishes *Smiles to Go.*

NOTES

Chapter 1

1 Jerry Spinelli, *Knots in My Yo-Yo String: The Autobiography of a Kid.* New York: Alfred A. Knopf, 1998, p. 67.

2 Ibid., p. 103.

3 Ibid., p. 64.

4 "Author Biography: Jerry Spinelli." BookBrowse: Your Guide to Exceptional Books, June 1, 2002. http://www.bookbrowse.com/biographies/index.cfm?author_number=455.

5 Jerry Spinelli, "Jerry Spinelli." AOL Kids Reads.

6 Spinelli, *Knots in My Yo-Yo String*, p. 86.

7 "Transcript of Authors Live with Jerry Spinelli." Teacher Vision, February 26, 2002. http://www.teachervision.fen.com/award-winners/authors/10140.html.

8 Spinelli, *Knots in My Yo-Yo String*, pp. 85–86.

Chapter 2

1 Don Gallo, "Jerry Spinelli." Authors 4 Teens. http://www.authors4teens.com/introduction.jsp?authorid=jspinelli.

2 "Authors Live with Jerry Spinelli," http://www.teachervision.fen.com/award-winners/authors/10140.html.

3 Raymond P. Kettel, "An Interview with Jerry Spinelli: Thoughts on Teaching Writing in the Classroom," *English Journal* (1994): p. 61.

4 Spinelli, "Jerry Spinelli." http://aol.kidsreads.com/authors/au-spinelli-jerry.asp.

5 Jennifer Brown, "Homer on George Street," *Publishers Weekly*, July 17, 2000. http://www.publishersweekly.com/article/CA168482.html.

6 "Jerry Spinelli Favorite Book . . ." *The Washington Post* (2003).

7 Kettel, "Interview with Jerry Spinelli," p. 61.

8 Diana L. Winarski, "Writing: Spinelli-style," *Teaching PreK–8.* Vol. 27, no. 2 (1996): p. 42.

Chapter 3

1 "The Gettysburgian: The Student Newspaper of Gettysburg College." Gettysburg College, http://www.gettysburg.edu/library/resources/db/splash/g/gettysburgian.dot.

2 "Gettysburg College MS-007: The Papers of Jerry Spinelli, Class of 1963." Gettysburg College. http://gettysburg.edu/special_collections/collections/manuscripts/collections/ms007.

3 "Gettysburg College, homepage." Gettysburg College. http://www.gettysburg.edu.

4 "Graduate Programs at the Writing Seminars." Johns Hopkins

University. http://www.jhu.edu/writingseminars/mfa/.

5 Spinelli, *Knots in My Yo-Yo String*, p. 12.

6 Beth Sneller, "'03 Reading Program to Feature 3 Authors," *Daily Herald,* January 5, 2003.

7 Winarski, "Writing: Spinelli-style," p. 42.

8 Spinelli, "Jerry Spinelli." http://aol.kidsreads.com/authors/au-spinelli-jerry.asp.

9 Kari Hartman, "Author enthralls young readers." *Daily Herald*, February 5, 2003.

10 Winarski, "Writing: Spinelli-style," p. 42.

11 Matthew Tully, "Maniac Magee's Author Tells Kids He Learned a Lot from Failure," Knight Ridder/Tribune News Service, April 20, 1994.

12 Ibid.

13 Winarski, "Writing: Spinelli-style," p. 43.

14 Ibid.

15 Brown, "Homer on George Street."

16 Winarski, "Writing: Spinelli-style," p. 43

17 Ibid.

Chapter 4

1 Tully, "Maniac Magee's Author."

2 Karen S. Roberts, "'Write What You Care About': Advice for Young Writers from Jerry Spinelli," *Writing.* Vol. 22, no. 3 (1999): p. 11.

3 Laura Zahn Pohl, "Naperville Schoolkids Hear Tales of 'Heroes'; District 203 plays host to 3

authors," *Chicago Tribune*, February 7, 2003.

4 Brown, "Homer on George Street."

5 Spinelli, "Jerry Spinelli," http://aol.kidsreads.com/authors/au-spinelli-jerry.asp.

6 Brown, "Homer on George Street."

7 Ibid.

8 John Keller, "Jerry Spinelli," *The Horn Book Magazine*, July/August 1991, p. 435.

9 Ibid.

10 Spinelli, "Jerry Spinelli," http://aol.kidsreads.com/authors/au-spinelli-jerry.asp.

11 Jerry Spinelli, *Space Station Seventh Grade*. Boston: Little, Brown, 1982, p. 21.

12 Jerry Spinelli, "Catching Maniac Magee," *The Reading Teacher*. Vol. 45, no. 3 (1991): p. 176.

13 Mona Kerby, "Jerry Spinelli." The Author Corner, April 19, 2000. http://www.carr.org/authco/spinelli-j.htm.

14 "Review of *Space Station Seventh Grade*," *Kirkus Reviews.* BCCLS. http://web2bccls.org/web2/tramp2.exe/see_record.

15 Kettel, "Interview with Jerry Spinelli," p. 61.

16 Roberts, "'Write What You Care About,'" p. 11.

Chapter 5

1 Donald R. Gallo, *Speaking for Ourselves*. Urbana, Illinois: National Council of Teachers of English, 1990, p. 198.

2 Patricia M. Newman, "Who Wrote That? Featuring Jerry Spinelli," *California Kids!* December 2003.

http://www.patriciamnewman.com/spinelli.html.

3 Sneller, "'03 Reading Program to Feature 3 Authors." http://goliath.ecnext.com/coms2/gi_0199-901525/03-reading-program-to-feature.html.

4 Spinelli, "Catching Maniac Magee," p. 176.

5 "Review of *Who Put That Hair in My Toothbrush?" Children's Literature.* Barnes and Noble. http://search.barnesandnoble.com/Who-Put-That-Hair-in-My-Toothbrush/Jerry-Spinelli/e/9780316806879.

6 David Gale, "Review of *Who Put That Hair in My Toothbrush?" School Library Journal.* Barnes and Noble. http://search.barnesandnoble.com/Who-Put-That-Hair-in-My-Toothbrush/Jerry-Spinelli/e/9780316806879.

7 Spinelli, *Knots in My Yo-Yo String,* p. 15.

8 "Review of *Jason and Marceline," Publishers Weekly.* Barnes and Noble. http://search.barnesand-noble.com/Jason-and-Marceline/Jerry-Spinelli/e/9780316806626.

9 "Review of *Jason and Marceline," Children's Literature.* Barnes and Noble. http://search.barnesand-noble.com/Jason-and-Marceline/Jerry-Spinelli/e/9780316806626.

10 "Review of *Jason and Marceline," School Library Journal.* http://search.barnesandnoble.com/Jason-and-Marceline/Jerry-Spinelli/e/9780316806626.

11 "Review of *Dump Days," Publishers Weekly.* Barnes and Noble. http://search.barnesandnoble.com/Dump-Days/Jerry-Spinelli/e/9780316807067/?itm=1.

12 "Review of *The Bathwater Gang," School Library Journal.* Barnes and Noble. http://search.barnesandnoble.com/Bathwater-Gang/Jerry-Spinelli/e/9780316014427/?itm=1.

13 Winarski, "Writing: Spinelli-style," p. 43.

14 Keller, "Jerry Spinelli." p. 435.

Chapter 6

1 Spinelli, "Catching Maniac Magee," p. 174

2 Ibid.

3 Ibid.

4 Kerby, "Jerry Spinelli," http://www.carr.org/authco/spinelli-j.htm.

5 Spinelli, "Catching Maniac Magee," p.174

6 Brown, "Homer on George Street."

7 Ibid.

8 Spinelli, "Catching Maniac Magee," p. 174

9 Jerry Spinelli, "Newbery Medal Acceptance," *The Horn Book Magazine*, July/August 1991, p. 431.

10 Kettel, "An Interview with Jerry Spinelli," p. 61.

11 Spinelli, "Catching Maniac Magee," p. 174

12 Ibid.

13 "Review of *Maniac Magee," Publishers Weekly.* Barnes and Noble. http://search.barnesandnoble.com/booksearch/results.asp?WRD=maniac+magee.

14 "Review of *Maniac Magee," School Library Journal.* Barnes and Noble. http://search.barnesandnoble.com/booksearch/results.asp?WRD=maniac+magee.

15 "About the Newbery Medal." American Library Association. http://www.ala.org/ala/alsc/awardsscholarships/literaryawds/newberymedal/aboutnewbery/aboutnewbery.htm.

16 Mary Blandin Bauer, "Choosing the Newbery Winner," *The Washington Post*, May 12, 1991.

17 Ibid.

18 Spinelli, "Newbery Medal Acceptance," p. 427.

19 Ibid.

20 Bauer, "Choosing the Newbery Winner."

21 Spinelli, "Newbery Medal Acceptance," p. 426.

22 Kerby, "Jerry Spinelli," http://www.carr.org/authco/spinelli-j.htm.

Chapter 7

1 Roberts, "Write What You Care About," p. 11.

2 "Review of *There's a Girl in My Hammerlock*," *Publishers Weekly*. Barnes and Noble. http://search.barnesandnoble.com/Theres-A-Girl-in-My-Hammerlock/Jerry-Spinelli/e/9781416939375/?itm=1.

3 Susan Knorr, "Review of *There's a Girl in My Hammerlock*," *School Library Journal*. http://search.barnesandnoble.com/Theres-A-Girl-in-My-Hammerlock/Jerry-Spinelli/e/9781416939375/?itm=1.

4 Pamela K. Bomboy, "Review of *Report to the Principal's Office*," *School Library Journal*. Barnes and Noble. http://search.barnesandnoble.com/Report-to-the-Principals-Office/Jerry-Spinelli/e/9780590462778/?itm=1.

5 Roberts, "Write What You Care About," p. 11.

6 "Review of *Fourth Grade Rats*," *Publishers Weekly*. Barnes and Noble. http://search.barnesandnoble.com/Fourth-Grade-Rats/Spinelli/e/9780590442442/?itm=1.

7 David Seidman, *Jerry Spinelli*. New York: Rosen, 2004, p. 71.

8 "Review of *The Bathwater Gang Gets Down to Business*," *Booklist*. Barnes and Noble. http://search.barnesandnoble.com/The-Bathwater-Gang-Gets-down-to-Business/Jerry-Spinelli/e/9780316808088/?itm=1.

9 Brown, "Homer on George Street."

10 Jerry Spinelli, *Tooter Pepperday*. New York: Random House, 1995, pp. 13–14.

11 "Review of *Tooter Pepperday*," *Children's Literature*. Barnes and Noble. http://search.barnesand-noble.com/Tooter-Pepperday/Jerry-Spinelli/e/9780679947028/?itm=3.

12 Mary Harris Veeder, "Review of *Tooter Pepperday*," *Booklist*. Amazon.com. http://www.amazon.com/Tooter-Pepperday-Stepping-Stone-paper/dp/0679847022/ref=sr_1_1?ie=UTF8&s=books&qid=1224875513&sr=1-1.

13 Pamela K. Bomboy, "Review of *Tooter Pepperday*," *School Library Journal*. Barnes and Noble. http://search.barnesandnoble.com/Tooter-Pepperday/Jerry-Spinelli/e/9780679947028/?itm=3

14 Seidman, *Jerry Spinelli*, p. 71.

15 Lisa Smith Lindenhurst, "Review of *Blue Ribbon Blues*," *School Library Journal*. Barnes and Noble.

http://search.barnesandnoble.com/
Blue-Ribbon-Blues/Jerry-Spinelli/
e/9780679887539/?itm=1.

16 "Review of *Tooter Pepperday*,"
Horn Book Magazine. Amazon.
com. http://www.amazon.com/
Tooter-Tale-Ribbon-Blues-Stepping.

17. "Review of *Crash*," *Publishers
Weekly*. Barnes and Noble. http://
search.barnesandnoble.com/Crash/
Jerry-Spinelli/e/9780679885504/
?itm=1.

18 "Review of *Crash*," *Children's
Literature*. Barnes and Noble. http://
search.barnesandnoble.com/Crash/
Jerry-Spinelli/e/9780679885504/
?itm=1.

19 Connie Tyrell Burns, "Review of
Crash," *School Library Journal*.
Barnes and Noble. http://search.
barnesandnoble.com/Crash/
Jerry-Spinelli/e/9780679885504/
?itm=1.

20 Steven Engelfried, "Review of *The
Library Card*," *School Library
Journal*. Barnes and Noble.
http://search.barnesandnoble.
com/Library-Card/Spinelli/
e/9780590386333/?itm=1.

21 "Review of *The Library Card*,"
Children's Literature. Barnes and
Noble. http://search.barnesand-
noble.com/Library-Card/Spinelli/
e/9780590386333/?itm=1.

22 "Review of *The Library Card*,"
Publishers Weekly. Barnes and
Noble. http://search.barnesand-
noble.com/Library-Card/Spinelli/
e/9780590386333/?itm=1.

23 Tim Rausch, "Review of *Wringer*,"
School Library Journal. Barnes
and Noble. http://search.barnesand-
noble.com/Wringer/Jerry-Spinelli/
e/9780064405782/?itm=1.

24 "Review of *Wringer*," *Children's
Literature*. Barnes and Noble.
http://search.barnesandnoble.
com/Wringer/Jerry-Spinelli/
e/9780064405782/?itm=1.

25 "Review of *Wringer*," *Kirkus
Reviews*. Barnes and Noble.
http://search.barnesandnoble.
com/Wringer/Jerry-Spinelli/
e/9780064405782/?itm=1.

26 Benjamin Cheever, "Pigeon
English," *The New York Times Book
Review*, November 16, 1997.

27 Roberts, " 'Write What You Care
About,' " p. 11.

28 "Review of *Knots in My Yo-
Yo String*," *Publishers Weekly*.
Barnes and Noble. http://search.
barnesandnoble.com/Knots-in-
My-Yo-Yo-String/Jerry-Spinelli/
e/9780679887911/?itm=1.

29 Susie Wilde, "Review of *Knots
in My Yo-Yo String*," *Children's
Literature*. Barnes and Noble. http://
search.barnesandnoble.com/Knots-
in-My-Yo-Yo-String/Jerry-Spinelli/
e/9780679887911/?itm=1.

30 Peter Sieruta, "*Knots in My Yo-Yo
String: The Autobiography of a
Kid*," *The Horn Book Magazine*.
Vol. 75, no.1 (1999), p. 88.

31 Brown, "Homer on George Street."

32 Stephen Del Vecchio, "For Kids,"
Teacher Magazine. Vol. 12, no.7
(2001), pp. 51–53.

33 Brown, "Homer on George Street."

34 "Review of *Stargirl*," *Publishers
Weekly*. Barnes and Noble. http://
search.barnesandnoble.com/book
search/results.asp?WRD=stargirl.

35 Diana Mitchell, "Review of
Stargirl," *The ALAN Review*.
Barnes and Noble. http://search.

barnesandnoble.com/booksearch/
results.asp?WRD=stargirl.

36 Kerby, "Jerry Spinelli," http://www.
carr.org/authco/spinelli-j.htm.

37 "Review of *Loser,*" *Book Magazine,*
no. 24 (September 1, 2002), p. 40.

38 Matthew Weaver, "Review
of *Loser,*" *VOYA.* Barnes and
Noble. http://search.barnes
andnoble.com/Loser/Jerry-Spinelli/
e/9780060540746/?itm=1.

39 "Review of *My Daddy and Me,*"
Publishers Weekly. Barnes and
Noble. http://search.barnes
andnoble.com/My-Daddy-and-Me/
Jerry-Spinelli/e/9780553113037/
?itm=1.

40 "Review of *My Daddy and Me,*"
Children's Literature. Barnes
and Noble. http://search.barnesand
noble.com/My-Daddy-and-Me/
Jerry-Spinelli/e/9780553113037/
?itm=1.

41 "Review of *My Daddy and Me,*"
Kirkus. Barnes and Noble. http://
search.barnesandnoble.com/My-
Daddy-and-Me/Jerry-Spinelli/
e/9780553113037/?itm=1.

42 "What's It About Jerry Spinelli?"
Scholastic Scope. Vol. 52, no. 16
(2004), pp. 12–13.

43 Ibid.

44 Steve Rasmussen, "Review of
Milkweed," *The ALAN Review.*
Barnes and Noble. http://www.
search.barnesandnoble.com/
booksearch.

45 Winarski, "Writing: Spinelli-style,"
p. 44.

Chapter 8

1 Chetra Kotzas, "Eileen Spinelli:
Poetic Living," *Sprouts* (2005), pp.
4–5.

2 Kerby, "Jerry Spinelli," http://www.
carr.org/authco/spinelli-j.htm.

3 Brown, "Homer on George Street."

4 Winarski, "Writing: Spinelli-style,"
p. 44.

5 Roberts, "'Write What You Care
About,'" p. 11.

6 Winarski, "Writing: Spinelli-style,"
p. 43.

7 Spinelli, "Newbery Medal
Acceptance," p. 427.

8 Brown, "Homer on George Street."

9 Kettel, "Interview with Jerry
Spinelli," p. 61.

10 "Summer Reading Coalition
Announces First Citywide Reading
Campaign to Benefit Teens," *PR
Newswire* (June 1, 2001).

11 Kari Hartman, "Author Enthralls
Young Readers," *Daily Herald*,
February 5, 2003.

12 Seidman, *Jerry Spinelli.* p. 72.

13 Brown, "Homer on George Street."

14 Roberts, "'Write What You Care
About,'" p. 11.

15 Brown, "Homer on George Street."

16 Hartman, "Author Enthralls Young
Readers."

17 "Authors Live with Jerry Spinelli,"
http://www.teachervision.fen.com/
award-winners/authors/10140.html.

18 Roberts, "'Write What You Care
About,'" p. 11.

19 Kerby, "Jerry Spinelli," http://
www.carr.org/authco/spinelli-j.htm.

20 Seidman, *Jerry Spinelli*, p. 71.

21 Kerby, "Jerry Spinelli," http://
www.carr.org/authco/spinelli-j.htm.

22 "Authors Live with Jerry Spinelli,"
http://www.teachervision.fen.com/
award-winners/authors/10140.html.

23 "Jerry Spinelli, Class of 1963," Gettysburg College http://www. gettysburg.edu/library/news/ exhibits/read.dot.

24 Newman, "Who Wrote That? Featuring Jerry Spinelli," http:// www.patriciamnewman.com/ spinelli.html.

25 Kerby, "Jerry Spinelli," http:// www.carr.org/authco/spinelli-j. htm.

26 Roberts, "'Write What You Care About,'" p. 11.

27 Kettel, "Interview with Jerry Spinelli," p. 61.

28 Ibid.

29 "Authors Live with Jerry Spinelli," http://www.teachervision.fen. com/award-winners/authors/10140. html.

30 Kettel, "Interview with Jerry Spinelli," p. 61.

31 Ibid.

32 Ibid.

Chapter 9

1 Roberts, "'Write What You Care About,'" p. 11.

2 Dave McNary, "'Geeks' guy to get 'Girl' for Par, Nick," *Daily Variety*, September 28, 2004. http:// findarticles.com/p/articles/mi_ hb5143/is_/ai_n18603436.

3 "Author Biography: Jerry Spinelli," http://www.bookbrowse.com/biogra phies/index.cfm?author_number=455.

4 Spinelli, "Jerry Spinelli," http://aol. kidsreads.com/authors/au-spinelli- jerry.asp.

WORKS BY JERRY SPINELLI

1982 *Space Station Seventh Grade*

1984 *Who Put That Hair in My Toothbrush?*

1985 *Night of the Whale*

1986 *Jason and Marceline*

1988 *Dump Days*

1990 *Maniac Magee*; *The Bathwater Gang*; *There's a Girl in My Hammerlock*

1991 *Fourth Grade Rats*; *Report to the Principal's Office*

1992 *The Bathwater Gang Gets Down to Business*; *Who Ran My Underwear Up the Flagpole?*; *Do the Funky Pickle*

1993 *Picklemania*

1995 *Tooter Pepperday*

1996 *Crash*

1997 *Wringer*; *The Library Card*; *Blue Ribbon Blues: A Tooter Tale*

1998 *Knots in My Yo-Yo String: The Autobiography of a Kid*

2000 *Stargirl*; *Loser*; *My Daddy and Me*

2003 *Milkweed*

2007 *Eggs*; *Love, Stargirl*

2008 *Smiles to Go*

POPULAR BOOKS

CRASH

John "Crash" Coogan is a typical tough guy. He is the complete opposite of the gentle vegetarian Quaker Penn Webb. He torments Penn, but after his beloved grandfather suffers a stroke, Crash finds that he and Penn have a lot in common and the two boys forge a friendship.

LOSER

Since the first grade, the kids at school have called Donald Zinkoff a loser. He is always happy, loves school, and wears a strange giraffe hat. Donald's courage in the wake of a tragedy shows everyone that he isn't a loser after all.

MANIAC MAGEE

Jeffrey Lionel Magee is an orphan who runs everywhere. When he finally stops running, he is in the town of Two Mills, Pennsylvania, where a black family and a rivalry between the blacks and whites in town await him. This book won the Newbery Medal in 1991.

STARGIRL

Leo Borlock falls in love with the ever-optimistic Stargirl Carraway, a quirky cheerleader. Trouble comes when Stargirl's enthusiasm is blamed for a big loss by the school during a football game. Can Stargirl and Leo be what everyone wants them to be and still be together?

WRINGER

Palmer LaRue dreads his tenth birthday. When boys turn 10 in his town, they become "wringers," participating in the annual pigeon shoot by wringing the necks of the injured birds. Palmer befriends a pigeon with personality and struggles to be the tough guy everyone thinks he is and still be himself.

POPULAR CHARACTERS

DONALD ZINKOFF

Donald is labeled a loser when his clumsiness costs the team a crucial game. At first, he doesn't mind and grins at those who tease him. Eventually the teasing does begin to bother him. With the love and support of his family, Donald is able to move past the "loser" label and let his true self shine through.

JEFFREY "MANIAC" MAGEE

Jeffrey is an orphan who runs into the town of Two Mills one day and begins a legend. He can hit a frog ball, run along the train tracks, and untangle the most stubborn knots. Just as naturally, he manages to unite a town divided along color lines and find a family.

JOHN "CRASH" COOGAN

Crash is every bully you've ever heard of who torments the kids who stand out because they are different. Crash learns that he is not so different from the kids he once tortured and that there is much more to people than what is on the surface.

PALMER LARUE

When Palmer turns nine, he begins his career as a tough kid, but he has a big secret. He does not want to be a wringer in the annual pigeon shoot, and he has a pigeon as a pet. Palmer struggles to balance his tough-guy life with the secret he is hiding in his bedroom.

STARGIRL CARAWAY

Stargirl is an unusual new addition to Mica High School. She dropped her given name, Susan, and changes her name to suit her mood. She keeps a pet rat, plays ukulele, and cheers when the opposing team scores. When this unusual girl is pressured to become just like the rest of the kids at her school, she can't seem to get it right.

MAJOR AWARDS

1990 *Maniac Magee* wins Boston Globe/Horn Book Award.

1991 *Maniac Magee* is awarded the Newbery Medal.

1996 *Crash* is listed as an American Library Association Best Book for Young Adults and as one of the *School Library Journal* Best Books.

1997 *Crash* is listed as an American Library Association Best Book for Young Adults; *Wringer* is listed as one of the *School Library Journal* Best Books.

1998 *Wringer* becomes a Newbery Honor book.

2001 *Stargirl* is listed as an American Library Association Best Book for Young Adults.

2003 *Milkweed* wins the Golden Kite Award.

BIBLIOGRAPHY

Ameduri, Christine M., Molly Thomas, and Sidney G. Dreese. "MS-007: The Papers of Jerry Spinelli, Class of 1963," Gettysburg College Archives, February 2004. Available online. URL: http://www. gettysburg.edu/special_collections.

"Author Biography: Jerry Spinelli," BookBrowse.com. June 1, 2002. Available online. URL: http://www.bookbrowse.com/biographies/ index.cfm?author_number=455.

Bauer, Mary Blandin. "Choosing the Newbery Winner." *Washington Post*, May 12, 1991.

Brown, Jennifer. "Jerry Spinelli Homer on George Street." *Publishers Weekly.* Vol. 249, no. 29 (July 17, 2000): pp. 168–169.

Carroll, Pamela Sissi. "YA Authors' Insights about the Art of Writing." *English Journal* (January 2001): pp. 104–109.

Cheever, Benjamin. "Pigeon English." *New York Times Book Review* (November 16, 1997).

Del Vecchio, Stephen. "For Kids." *Teacher Magazine.* Vol. 12, no. 7 (April 1, 2001): pp. 51–53.

Gale, David. Review of *Night of the Whale. School Library Journal.* Barnes and Noble. November 17, 2006. Available online. URL: http://www.bn.com.

Gallo, Donald R. *Speaking for Ourselves.* Urbana, Illinois: National Council of Teachers of English, 1990.

Hartman, Kari. "Author enthralls young readers." *Daily Herald,* February 5, 2003. Available online. URL: http://www.findarticles.com/p/ articles/mi_hb5273/is_/ai_n20744062

Hepler, Susan. Review of *The Bathwater Gang.* Barnes and Noble. November 17, 2006. Available online. URL: http://www.bn.com.

"Jerry Spinelli." *Contemporary Authors Online,* Gale 2006. Reproduced in *Biography Resource Center.* Farmington Hills, Mich.: Thomson Gale, 2006. Available online. URL: http://galenet.galegroup.com/servlet/ BioRC

"Jerry Spinelli." *Major Authors and Illustrators for Children and Young Adults,* 2nd ed. Gale Group, 2002. Reproduced in *Biography*

Resource Center. Farmington Hills, Mich.: Thomson Gale, 2006. Available online. URL: http://galenet.galegroup.com/servlet/ BioRC

"Jerry Spinelli's Favorite Book…" *Washington Post.* September 30, 2003. Available online. URL: http://www.highbeam.com/doc/1P2-297113. html

Keller, John. "Jerry Spinelli." *Horn Book Magazine,* July/August 1991, pp. 433–436.

Kerby, Mona. "Jerry Spinelli." The Author Corner. April 19, 2000. Available online. URL: http://www.carr.org/authco/spinelli-j.htm.

Kettel, Raymond P. "An Interview with Jerry Spinelli: Thoughts on teaching writing in the classroom." *English Journal.* Vol. 83, no. 5 (September 1994): p. 61.

Kotzas, Chetra. "Eileen Spinelli Poetic Living." *Sprouts* (Fall 2005): pp. 4–5.

McNary, Dave. " 'Geeks' Guy to Get 'Girl' for Paramount Pictures, Nickelodeon Films." *Daily Variety* (September 28, 2004). Available online. URL: http://findarticles.com/p/articles/mi_hb5143/is_/ai_ n18603436

"Meet the Author: Jerry Spinelli." *Edu Place.* Available online. URL: http://www.eduplace.com/kids/tnc/mtai/spinelli.html.

Newman, Patricia M. "Who Wrote That? Featuring Jerry Spinelli." *California Kids!* December 2003. Available online. URL: http:// www.patriciamnewman.com/spinelli.html.

Pohl, Laura Zahn. "Naperville Schoolkids Hear Tales of 'Heroes'; District 203 Plays Host to 3 Authors." *Chicago Tribune,* February 7, 2003.

Review of *Dump Days.* May 1988. *Publishers Weekly.* Barnes and Noble. November 17, 2006. Available online. URL: http://www.bn.com.

Review of *Jason and Marceline. Children's Literature.* Barnes and Noble. November 17, 2006. Available online. URL: http://www.bn.com

Review of *Jason and Marceline. Publishers Weekly.* Barnes and Noble. November 17, 2006. Available online. URL: http://www.bn.com.

Review of *Maniac Magee. Publishers Weekly* Barnes and Noble. Available online. URL: http://www.bn.com.

Review of *Maniac Magee. School Library Journal.* Barnes and Noble. Available online. URL: http://www.bn.com.

Review of *Space Station Seventh Grade. Kirkus Reviews.* 1984. Available online. URL: http://www.kirkusreviews.com.

Review of *Who Put That Hair in My Toothbrush? Children's Literature.* Barnes and Noble. November 17, 2006. Available online. URL: http://www.bn.com.

Review of *Who Put That Hair in My Toothbrush? Publishers Weekly.* Barnes and Noble. November 17, 2006. Available online. URL: http://www.bn.com.

Roberts, Karen S. "'Write What You Care About': Advice for Young Writers from Jerry Spinelli." *Writing.* Vol. 22, no. 3 (November/ December 1999): p. 11.

Seidman, David. *Jerry Spinelli.* New York: Rosen, 2004.

Sieruta, Peter D. Review of *Knots in My Yo-Yo String: The Autobiography of a Kid. Horn Book Magazine.* Vol. 75, no. 1 (January/February 1999): p. 87.

Sneller, Beth. "'03 Reading Program to Feature 3 Authors." *Daily Herald,* January 5, 2003.

Spinelli, Jerry. "Catching Maniac Magee." *Reading Teacher.* Vol. 45, no. 3 (November 1991): pp. 174–176.

Spinelli, Jerry. "Jerry Spinelli." Kidsreads.com. Available online. URL: http://aol.kidsreads.com/authors/au-spinelli-jerry.asp.

Spinelli, Jerry. "Jerry Spinelli Class of 1963." *Read.* Gettysburg College. November 27, 2006. Available online. URL: http://www.gettysburg. edu/library/news/exhibits/read.dot.

Spinelli, Jerry. *Knots in My Yo-Yo String: The Autobiography of a Kid.* New York: Alfred A. Knopf, 1998.

Spinelli, Jerry. "Newbery Medal Acceptance." *Horn Book Magazine,* July/ August 1991, pp. 426–432.

Spinelli, Jerry. *Who Put That Hair in My Toothbrush?* Boston: Little, Brown, 1984.

"Spotlight on Jerry Spinelli." Teachers@Random. Available online. URL: http://www.randomhouse.com/teachers/authors/results. pperl?authorid=29311.

"Transcript of Authors Live with Jerry Spinelli." TeacherVision. February 26, 2002. Available online. URL: http://www.teachervision.fen.com/ award-winners/authors/10140.html.

Tully, Matthew. "Maniac Magee's Author Tells Kids He Learned a Lot from Failure." Knight Ridder/Tribune News Service (April 20, 1994). Available online. URL: http://www.accessmylibrary.com/ coms2/summary_0286-5513760_ITM.

Unsworth, Robert. Review of *Jason and Marceline, School Library Journal.* Barnes and Noble. November 17, 2006. Available online. URL: http://www.bn.com.

Warsmith, Stephanie. "Stargirl Founder Helps Younger Students Shine." *Akron Beacon Journal*, May 28, 2006.

"What's It About, Jerry Spinelli?" *Scholastic Scope.* Vol. 52, no. 16 (2004), p. 12.

Winarski, Diana L. "Writing: Spinelli-style." *Teaching Pre K-8.* Vol. 27, no. 2 (October 1996), pp. 42–44.

FURTHER READING

Books

McGinty, Alice. *Meet Jerry Spinelli*. New York: PowerKids Press, 2003.

Micklos, John Jr. *Jerry Spinelli: Master Teller of Teen Tales*. New York: Rosen, 2007.

Web Sites

THE AUTHOR CORNER

http://www.carr.org/authco

> Mona Kerby's Web site The Author Corner is billed as "a place to meet authors and illustrators of children's and young adult books." It was created to provide this information for students from grades 2 through 10.

BARNES AND NOBLE

http://www.bn.com

> Visitors to Barnes and Noble's online store can enter Jerry Spinelli's name in the search box to find all books and media adaptations by and about the author.

JERRY SPINELLI'S OFFICIAL SITE

http://www.jerryspinelli.com

> Jerry Spinelli's official Web site includes information about his books, an FAQ page that covers everything from advice for writers to information about Spinelli's family, a news section of the latest happenings with Spinelli's books, a schedule of upcoming events, and information on creating a Stargirl Society. Visitors are also treated to activities like a Spinelli crossword puzzle on the "Fun Stuff" page.

KIDS READS

http://www.kidsreads.com

> The Kids Reads Web site (AOL keyword: Bookworm) publishes information about favorite books and authors. Its special features include trivia and games such as word scrambles and word

searches. Kids Reads also has an archive of reviews of books featured on the site.

TEACHERVISION

http://www.teachervision.fen.com

The TeacherVision Web site has information on authors' books, interviews with authors, and lesson plans and printable activities for use in classrooms. Visitors to the site will find a recent interview with Spinelli about his book *Milkweed.*

PICTURE CREDITS

INDEX

ABOUT THE CONTRIBUTOR

TRACEY BAPTISTE is a former elementary school teacher and textbook editor. She now writes books for children and young adults. Her first young adult novel, *Angel's Grace*, was published in 2005. Her nonfiction titles include *Overcoming Prejudice* and *Being a Leader and Making Decisions*. You can read more about Ms. Baptiste at http://www.traceybaptiste.com.

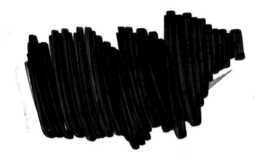